T0188795

Cybersecurity Risk Management

Mastering the Fundamentals Using the NIST Cybersecurity Framework

Cybersecurity Risk Management

Mastering the Fundamentals Using the NIST Cybersecurity Framework

Cynthia Brumfield
*Cybersecurity analyst, writer
and President of DCT Associates,
Washington, D.C., USA*

with

Brian Haugli
*Managing Partner,
SideChannel, Boston, USA*

Registered Office

John Wiley & Sons, Inc., 111 River Street, Hoboken, NJ 07030, USA

Editorial Office

The Atrium, Southern Gate, Chichester, West Sussex, PO19 8SQ, UK

For details of our global editorial offices, customer services, and more information about Wiley products visit us at www.wiley.com.

Wiley also publishes its books in a variety of electronic formats and by print-on-demand. Some content that appears in standard print versions of this book may not be available in other formats.

Library of Congress Cataloging-in-Publication Data

Names: Brumfield, Cynthia, author. | Haugli, Brian, author. | John Wiley & Sons, publisher.

Title: Cybersecurity risk management : mastering the fundamentals using the NIST cybersecurity framework / Cynthia Brumfield, Brian Haugli.

Description: Hoboken, NJ : John Wiley & Sons, Inc., 2022. | Includes bibliographical references and index.

Identifiers: LCCN 2021024435 (print) | LCCN 2021024436 (ebook) | ISBN 9781119816287 (hardback) | ISBN 9781119816294 (pdf) | ISBN 9781119816300 (epub) | ISBN 9781119816348 (ebook)

Subjects: LCSH: Computer security--Risk management.

Classification: LCC QA76.9.A25 B82 2022 (print) | LCC QA76.9.A25 (ebook) | DDC 005.8--dc23

LC record available at https://lccn.loc.gov/2021024435

LC ebook record available at https://lccn.loc.gov/2021024436

Cover image: © Henrik5000/Getty Images

Cover design by Wiley

Set in 11.5/13pt BemboStd by Integra Software Services, Pondicherry, India

SKY10057325_101123

This book is dedicated to
Lloyd and Delma Brumfield,
who gave me everything I needed,
and then some.

Contents

Academic Foreword   **xiii**

Acknowledgments   **xv**

Preface – Overview of the NIST Framework   **xvii**

Background on the Framework   xviii
Framework Based on Risk Management   xix
The Framework Core   xix
Framework Implementation Tiers   xxi
Framework Profile   xxii
Other Aspects of the Framework Document   xxiii
Recent Developments At Nist   xxiii

CHAPTER 1
Cybersecurity Risk Planning and Management   **1**

Introduction   2
I.   What Is Cybersecurity Risk Management?   2
     A.   *Risk Management Is a Process*   3
II.   Asset Management   4
     A.   *Inventory Every Physical Device and System You Have and Keep the Inventory Updated*   5
     B.   *Inventory Every Software Platform and Application You Use and Keep the Inventory Updated*   9
     C.   *Prioritize Every Device, Software Platform, and Application Based on Importance*   10
     D.   *Establish Personnel Security Requirements Including Third-Party Stakeholders*   11
III.   Governance   13
     A.   *Make Sure You Educate Management about Risks*   13
IV.   Risk Assessment and Management   15
     A.   *Know Where You're Vulnerable*   15
     B.   *Identify the Threats You Face, Both Internally and Externally*   16
     C.   *Focus on the Vulnerabilities and Threats That Are Most Likely AND Pose the Highest Risk to Assets*   17
     D.   *Develop Plans for Dealing with the Highest Risks*   18

Summary   20
Chapter Quiz   20
Essential Reading on Cybersecurity Risk Management   22

CHAPTER 2
User and Network Infrastructure Planning and Management   23
   I.   Introduction   24
  II.   Infrastructure Planning and Management Is All about
       Protection, Where the Rubber Meets the Road   24
     A. *Identity Management, Authentication, and Access Control*   25
        1. Always Be Aware of Who Has Access to Which System,
            for Which Period of Time, and from Where the Access
            Is Granted   27
        2. Establish, Maintain, and Audit an Active Control List and
            Process for Who Can Physically Gain Access to Systems   28
        3. Establish Policies, Procedures, and Controls for Who
            Has Remote Access to Systems   28
        4. Make Sure That Users Have the Least Authority
            Possible to Perform Their Jobs and Ensure That at
            Least Two Individuals Are Responsible for a Task   29
        5. Implement Network Security Controls on All
            Internal Communications, Denying Communications
            among Various Segments Where Necessary   31
    A Word about Firewalls   31
        6. Associate Activities with a Real Person or a Single
            Specific Entity   32
        7. Use Single- or Multi-Factor Authentication Based
            on the Risk Involved in the Interaction   33
  III.   Awareness and Training   34
     A. *Make Sure That Privileged Users and Security Personnel*
        Understand Their Roles and Responsibilities   35
   IV.   Data Security   35
     A. *Protect the Integrity of Active and Archived Databases*   35
     B. *Protect the Confidentiality and Integrity of Corporate Data*
        Once It Leaves Internal Networks   36
     C. *Assure That Information Can Only Be Accessed by Those*
        Authorized to Do So and Protect Hardware and
        Storage Media   37
     D. *Keep Your Development and Testing Environments Separate*
        from Your Production Environment   38
     E. *Implement Checking Mechanisms to Verify Hardware Integrity*   39
   V.   Information Protection Processes and Procedures   39
     A. *Create a Baseline of IT and OT Systems*   40
     B. *Manage System Configuration Changes in a Careful,*
        Methodical Way   41
    A Word about Patch Management   42
     C. *Perform Frequent Backups and Test Your Backup*
        Systems Often   43

D. *Create a Plan That Focuses on Ensuring That Assets and Personnel Will Be Able to Continue to Function in the Event of a Crippling Attack or Disaster*   43

VI. Maintenance   44

A. *Perform Maintenance and Repair of Assets and Log Activities Promptly*   45

B. *Develop Criteria for Authorizing, Monitoring, and Controlling All Maintenance and Diagnostic Activities for Third Parties*   45

VII. Protective Technology   46

A. *Restrict the Use of Certain Types of Media On Your Systems*   46

B. *Wherever Possible, Limit Functionality to a Single Function Per Device (Least Functionality)*   47

C. *Implement Mechanisms to Achieve Resilience on Shared Infrastructure*   48

Summary   49

Chapter Quiz   50

Essential Reading on Network Management   51

CHAPTER 3
Tools and Techniques for Detecting Cyber Incidents   **53**

Introduction   54

What Is an Incident?   55

I. Detect   56

A. *Anomalies and Events*   56

1. Establish Baseline Data for Normal, Regular Traffic Activity and Standard Configuration for Network Devices   57

2. Monitor Systems with Intrusion Detection Systems and Establish a Way of Sending and Receiving Notifications of Detected Events; Establish a Means of Verifying, Assessing, and Tracking the Source of Anomalies   58

A Word about Antivirus Software   60

3. Deploy One or More Centralized Log File Monitors and Configure Logging Devices throughout the Organization to Send Data Back to the Centralized Log Monitor   61

4. Determine the Impact of Events Both Before and After they Occur   61

5. Develop a Threshold for How Many Times an Event Can Occur Before You Take Action   62

B. *Continuous Monitoring*   62

1. Develop Strategies for Detecting Breaches as Soon as Possible, Emphasizing Continuous Surveillance of Systems through Network Monitoring   63

2. Ensure That Appropriate Access to the Physical Environment Is Monitored, Most Likely through Electronic Monitoring or Alarm Systems   64

3. Monitor Employee Behavior in Terms of Both Physical and Electronic Access to Detect Unauthorized Access   65

4. Develop a System for Ensuring That Software Is Free of Malicious Code through Software Code Inspection and Vulnerability Assessments   65

5. Monitor Mobile Code Applications (e.g., Java Applets) for Malicious Activity by Authenticating the Codes' Origins, Verifying their Integrity, and Limiting the Actions they Can Perform   66

6. Evaluate a Provider's Internal and External Controls' Adequacy and Ensure they Develop and Adhere to Appropriate Policies, Procedures, and Standards; Consider the Results of Internal and External Audits   66

7. Monitor Employee Activity for Security Purposes and Assess When Unauthorized Access Occurs   67

8. Use Vulnerability Scanning Tools to Find Your Organization's Weaknesses   68

C. Detection Processes   68

1. Establish a Clear Delineation between Network and Security Detection, with the Networking Group and the Security Group Having Distinct and Different Responsibilities   69

2. Create a Formal Detection Oversight and Control Management Function; Define Leadership for a Security Review, Operational Roles, and a Formal Organizational Plan; Train Reviewers to Perform Their Duties Correctly and Implement the Review Process   70

3. Test Detection Processes Either Manually or in an Automated Fashion in Conformance with the Organization's Risk Assessment   71

4. Inform Relevant Personnel Who Must Use Data or Network Security Information about What Is Happening and Otherwise Facilitate Organizational Communication   71

5. Document the Process for Event Detection to Improve the Organization's Detection Systems   72

Summary   72

Chapter Quiz   73

Essential Reading for Tools and Techniques for Detecting a Cyberattack   74

CHAPTER 4
Developing a Continuity of Operations Plan   **75**

Introduction   77

A. One Size Does Not Fit All   77

I. Response   77

A. Develop an Executable Response Plan   79

B. Understand the Importance of Communications in Incident Response   80

    C.   *Prepare for Corporate-Wide Involvement During Some*
       Cybersecurity Attacks   81
  II. Analysis   82
    A.   *Examine Your Intrusion Detection System in Analyzing an*
       Incident   82
    B.   *Understand the Impact of the Event*   83
    C.   *Gather and Preserve Evidence*   84
    D.   *Prioritize the Treatment of the Incident Consistent with Your*
       Response Plan   84
    E.   *Establish Processes for Handling Vulnerability Disclosures*   85
  III. Mitigation   86
    A.   *Take Steps to Contain the Incident*   86
    B.   *Decrease the Threat Level by Eliminating or Intercepting*
       the Adversary as Soon as the Incident Occurs   87
    C.   *Mitigate Vulnerabilities or Designate Them as Accepted Risk*   88
  IV. Recover   88
    A.   *Recovery Plan Is Executed During or After a Cybersecurity*
       Incident   89
    B.   *Update Recovery Procedures Based on New Information as*
       Recovery Gets Underway   91
    C.   *Develop Relationships with Media to Accurately Disseminate*
       Information and Engage in Reputational Damage Limitation   92
Summary   92
Chapter Quiz   93
Essential Reading for Developing a Continuity of Operations Plan   94

CHAPTER 5
Supply Chain Risk Management   **95**
Introduction   96
  I. NIST Special Publication 800-161   96
  II. Software Bill of Materials   97
  III. NIST Revised Framework Incorporates Major
      Supply Chain Category   98
    A.   *Identify, Establish, and Assess Cyber Supply Chain Risk*
       Management Processes and Gain Stakeholder Agreement   98
    B.   *Identify, Prioritize, and Assess Suppliers and Third-Party*
       Partners of Suppliers   99
    C.   *Develop Contracts with Suppliers and Third-Party Partners*
       to Address Your Organization's Supply Chain Risk
       Management Goals   100
    D.   *Routinely Assess Suppliers and Third-Party Partners Using*
       Audits, Test Results, and Other Forms of Evaluation   101
    E.   *Test to Make Sure Your Suppliers and Third-Party Providers*
       Can Respond to and Recover from Service Disruption   102
Summary   103
Chapter Quiz   103
Essential Reading for Supply Chain Risk Management   104

CHAPTER 6
Manufacturing and Industrial Control Systems Security   **105**
Essential Reading on Manufacturing and Industrial
Control Security   110

Appendix A: Helpful Advice for Small Organizations
Seeking to Implement Some of the Book's Recommendations   **111**

Appendix B: Critical Security Controls Version 8.0 Mapped
to NIST CSF v1.1   **113**

Answers to Chapter Quizzes   **121**

Index   **131**

Academic Foreword

As a professor who has developed cybersecurity education programs for industry, academia, and the government, I know first-hand how difficult it can be for even advanced IT professionals to grasp the complex concepts in cybersecurity. In my role as Executive Director of the Center for Information Assurance and Cybersecurity at the University of Washington in Seattle, among other positions I hold, I have seen even the best and brightest of the nation's high-tech sector struggle when it comes to this still-new discipline. The difficulty is compounded by the varied missions that public, private, and academic organizations pursue.

My center at the University of Washington is a Center of Academic Excellence in both Cybersecurity Education and Research, so designated by the National Security Agency and the Department of Homeland Security. This honor means that we are well placed to help bridge the cybersecurity communications gaps that exist across crucial sectors of society: government, industry, and academia.

At the University of Washington, we take a pragmatic approach to equipping our students with the skills they need to enter the cybersecurity workforce. We emphasize critical thinking along with information management and technical skills so that we graduate 'breach-ready' students. Since there is no system that is 100% secure, we ingrain in our students the importance of having risk management tools in their toolkit, so they are equipped to make rational choices about what to protect and where to spend scarce cybersecurity dollars. We've found that the NIST Cybersecurity Framework is highly useful in conveying concepts in risk management.

The Framework does not offer step-by-step instruction on installing a firewall, for example, nor does it recommend any specific technology for, say, managing patch updates. Instead, it offers a way to comprehensively manage cybersecurity risks by drawing on the best-of-breed conceptual thinking from other risk management frameworks, informed by prevailing standards. It teaches our students how to think about solving a cybersecurity problem and that there is no 'one-size-fits-all' solution.

More importantly, NIST designed the Framework as a cybersecurity management tool to foster better communications among internal and external stakeholders. As a result, it bridges the communication gaps among silos, helping to create a common language to solve the growing number of cybersecurity problems. This book, with its practical approach to applying the Framework, should help students at all levels – undergraduate, graduate, and continuing education—become more Work-ready.

By walking the fine line between nitty-gritty technical discussions and high-level conceptual models, *Cybersecurity Risk Management: Mastering the Fundamentals using the NIST Cybersecurity Framework* should leave its readers with a new way of thinking about cybersecurity risk management. I hope that it also gives them the confidence to dive deeper into the growing number of cybersecurity disciplines that make up the cybersecurity field.

Barbara Endicott-Popovsky, Ph.D., CRISC
Executive Director, Center for Information Assurance and Cybersecurity
Professor, University of Washington
November 2021

Acknowledgments

This book is the culmination of at least eight years of research on how organizations can better position themselves to manage cybersecurity risk. My work on the material in this book began in 2013 when CSO Online commissioned me to document the development of what is now known as the NIST Cybersecurity Framework.

To accomplish this documentation, I attended all six of the workshops that led to the Framework's release in 2014, flying to universities around the country and talking to the world's leading cybersecurity experts for my CSO reports. A trade association also hired me to help industry executives understand cybersecurity. This client subsequently hired me to develop a series of courses to help train their workforce, particularly their non-cybersecurity technical personnel, in the best risk management practices using the NIST Cybersecurity Framework as a guide. (And I'm grateful that I was able to retain the rights to most of my work for this client.)

I've based the content of this book on the many discussions I have had with experts who have graciously given me their time over the years to explain how they manage risks in their organizations. Thanks to the following individuals in particular, whose skill and guidance helped bring many of the NIST concepts, so often abstract and high-level, down to earth and understandable to non-cybersecurity tech workers:

- Paul Anderson, Director of Corporate Information Services, Hubbard Broadcasting,
- Howard Price, formerly CBCP/MBCI, Senior Manager, Business Continuity Planning Corporate Risk Management, The Walt Disney Company,
- Dan Ryan, formerly Vice President, Information Technology, Nexstar Broadcasting, Inc.; now Head of Information Technology at Standard Media Group LLC,
- Eric Winter, Vice President of Investigations and Technical Risk, Cox Enterprises,
- Mike Kelley, Vice President, Chief Information Security Officer, The E.W. Scripps Company,
- Jim Davis, formerly Director, Infrastructure & Service Delivery, Cox Media Group,

- Michael Funk, Director of Information Technology, Quincy Media, Inc., and
- Eric Neel, Director Information Technology Infrastructure, Hubbard Broadcasting

I owe a huge debt of gratitude to Wayne Pecena of Texas A&M University for his expert review of most of the written material in this book. Thanks, Wayne, for your kind, wise and knowledgeable input into the book, particularly your sage advice to small organizations.

I'm incredibly grateful to the other cybersecurity experts who lent their experience to the Voices of Experience commentary throughout the book, including Patrick Miller, Lesley Carhart, Jason Boswell, and Casey Ellis. Your generosity will help your peers and other IT professionals to make their organizations more secure.

Finally, thanks to the countless other cybersecurity experts who I have interviewed over the years. Your contributions to helping people understand how to apply complex risk management concepts in the real world are invaluable contributions to the field. Without you, this book would not be possible.

Cynthia Brumfield
May 2021

I would first thank Cynthia for bringing me into this project. My hope has always been to see the NIST Cybersecurity Framework adopted by any organization looking to better their security posture on a well-established national standard. This book will allow that to happen. I would also like to thank those CISOs that lent their Voices of Experience to bring out their practitioners' views: Omer Singer, Bill Roberts, Joe Klein, Helen Patton, Sounil Yu, Gary Hayslip, Mike Waters, and Eric Hussey. Lastly, thank you to my wife Kim and daughter Juli for all your support with everything we do.

Brian Haugli
May 2021

Preface – Overview of the NIST Framework

The National Institute of Standards and Technology (NIST), located in Gaithersburg, MD, is a US Department of Commerce division. It is assigned the job of promoting innovation and industrial competitiveness. It is a research organization filled with some of the world's leading scientists and has produced many Nobel Prize winners.

NIST has a wide-ranging mandate: develop federal patents, oversee over 1,300 Standard Reference Materials, run a scientific laboratory in Boulder, CO, and pursue innovation in encryption technologies, among other significant efforts. NIST is primarily a scientific and engineering organization and, as such, produces patents, technical breakthroughs, documentation, and recommendations through extensive consultation with experts in various areas. This scientific consensus approach often has impressive results that can be difficult for non-specialists to understand or apply.

The NIST Cybersecurity Framework resulted from an intensive one-year effort to synthesize cybersecurity experts' best thinking into a single "framework of frameworks" that can assure superior risk management. It's well-understood in the cybersecurity field that risks are constant and that the best approach to organizational cybersecurity is to manage those risks because no one can eliminate them.

The NIST Framework attempts to incorporate all the best various risk management and remediation practices into one coherent whole, an ambitious goal in the complex cybersecurity field. It is a multi-layered, spoke-and-wheel collection of ideas grouped along logical lines.

The Framework is conceptual and not technical, making it a challenge for many organizations to apply in the real world. It doesn't help that NIST specifically avoided any technical recommendations when developing the Framework. NIST instead chose to map its recommendations to a host of standards, or informative references, designed in-house and at other standards-setting bodies.

Despite its growing use among leading corporations, government offices, and non-profit organizations in the United States and worldwide, many non-cybersecurity professionals, and even some cybersecurity specialists, struggle with the practical application of the NIST Framework.

The following summary provides a broad overview of what the Framework is and how it's structured. Keep in mind that the rest of the book focuses on the much-needed practical guidance on applying the NIST Framework, which we hope even non-cybersecurity professionals will grasp and find useful.

BACKGROUND ON THE FRAMEWORK

In the face of growing concerns over the prospect of a devastating cyberattack on US critical infrastructure, President Barack Obama issued on February 12, 2013, Executive Order (EO) 13636 "Improving Critical Infrastructure Cybersecurity."[1] The EO aimed to create a "partnership with the owners and operators of critical infrastructure to improve cybersecurity information sharing and collaboratively develop and implement risk-based standards." To achieve that objective, the EO mandated that NIST develop within one year "a voluntary risk-based Cybersecurity Framework, a set of industry standards and best practices to help organizations manage cybersecurity risks."

To hammer out the Framework, NIST hosted five workshops at multiple universities involving thousands of domestic and international private- and government-sector participants. Finally, on February 12, 2014, NIST issued the *Framework for Improving Critical Infrastructure Cybersecurity*.[2] The Department of Homeland Security (DHS) currently considers 16 sectors to be critical infrastructure sectors, encompassing information technology, financial services, energy, communications, manufacturing, and many other central services.[3] However, NIST hopes that the Framework will be helpful to all organizations and anticipates that its application will extend beyond critical infrastructure.

Underscoring the "living" nature of the Framework, on April 16, 2018, NIST issued an update, Version 1.1.[4] The updated Framework features several additional subcategories, including an expansive new set of subcategories dealing with Supply Chain Risk, a timely addition as the protection of digital supply chains has taken center stage due to some recent damaging and high-profile supply chain attacks.

In developing the Framework, NIST wanted to ensure maximum flexibility of application. The final document is industry- and technology-neutral. It encompasses hundreds of standards. It is also international in scope.

---

[1]Executive Order No. 13636 – *Improving Critical Infrastructure Cybersecurity*, February 12, 2013, at https://www.whitehouse.gov/the-press-office/2013/02/12/executive-order-improving-critical-infrastructure-cybersecurity.

[2]NIST Cybersecurity Framework, https://www.nist.gov/cyberframework/framework.

[3]Cybersecurity and Infrastructure Security Agency, Critical Infrastructure Sectors, https://www.cisa.gov/critical-infrastructure-sectors.

[4]Cybersecurity Framework 1.1 https://www.nist.gov/cyberframework/framework.

NIST stresses that the Framework is not intended to replace any organization's existing cybersecurity program but is a tool to strengthen existing practices. Suppose an organization does not have a cybersecurity risk management program or set of cybersecurity practices in place? In that case, the Framework should serve as a good starting point for developing that program or those practices.

FRAMEWORK BASED ON RISK MANAGEMENT

NIST premised the entire Framework on the concept of risk management, which is "the ongoing process of identifying, assessing, and responding to risk," an approach that provides a dynamic implementation of the Framework's recommendations. Under a risk management approach, "organizations may choose to handle risk in different ways, including mitigating the risk, transferring the risk, avoiding the risk, or accepting the risk, depending on the potential impact to the delivery of critical services."[5]

The Framework consists of three parts: The Framework Core, the Framework Implementation, and the Framework Profile Tiers. The purpose of these three parts is to provide a "common language" that all organizations can use to understand, manage, and communicate their cybersecurity initiatives, both internally and externally, and can scale down or up to various parts of an organization as needed.

THE FRAMEWORK CORE

The Framework Core is a set of activities aimed at organizing cybersecurity initiatives to achieve specific outcomes. The Core has five functions: Identify, Protect, Detect, Respond, and Recover (Figure 0.1).

Within each of these functions are categories of activities. Within each category of activities are subcategories, and for each subcategory, there are informative references, usually standards, for helping to support the activities (Figure 0.2).

For example, one category under the function Identify is Asset Management (Figure 0.3). A subcategory of Asset Management is "Physical devices and systems within the organization are inventoried." For that subcategory, the Framework offers informative references that guide physical devices' inventory, mostly standards established by various technical standards-setting bodies. The complete listing of the Functions, Categories, Subcategories, and Informative References are in Appendix A of the final Framework Document on the NIST website.[6]

---

[5]NIST Framework, p. 5.
[6]See https://nvlpubs.nist.gov/nistpubs/CSWP/NIST.CSWP.04162018.pdf Appendix A.

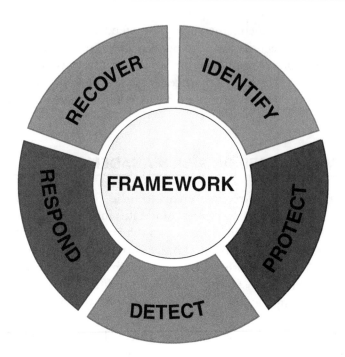

FIGURE 0.1   NIST Core Framework.

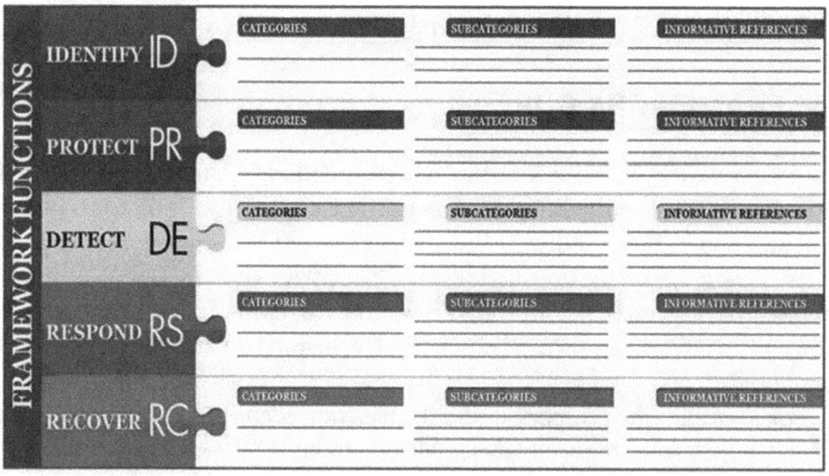

FIGURE 0.2   NIST Categories, Subcategories, and Informative References.

Although some organizations find the Framework Core, Categories, and Subcategories to be daunting, NIST intends them to be resources from which certain elements can be selected or examined, or used depending on the organization's unique configuration. NIST does not intend it to serve as a checklist of required activities. Nor are the Functions "intended to form a serial path, or lead to a static desired end state."

Function Unique Identifier	Function	Category Unique Identifier	Category
ID	Identify	ID.AM	Asset Management
		ID.BE	Business Environment
		ID.GV	Governance
		ID.RA	Risk Assessment
		ID.RM	Risk Management Strategy
		ID.SC	Supply Chain Risk Management
PR	Protect	PR.AC	Identity Management and Access Control
		PR.AT	Awareness and Training
		PR.DS	Data Security
		PR.IP	Information Protection Processes and Procedures
		PR.MA	Maintenance
		PR.PT	Protective Technology
DE	Detect	DE.AE	Anomalies and Events
		DE.CM	Security Continuous Monitoring
		DE.DP	Detection Processes
RS	Respond	RS.RP	Response Planning
		RS.CO	Communications
		RS.AN	Analysis
		RS.MI	Mitigation
		RS.IM	Improvements
RC	Recover	RC.RP	Recovery Planning
		RC.IM	Improvements
		RC.CO	Communications

FIGURE 0.3 NIST Functions and Categories.

FRAMEWORK IMPLEMENTATION TIERS

The Framework Implementation Tiers consist of four levels of "how an organization views cybersecurity risk and the processes in place to manage that risk." Although the levels are progressive in terms of rigor and sophistication from Tier 1 (partial) to Tier 4 (Adaptive), they are not "maturity" levels in terms of cybersecurity approaches. NIST based successful implementation on the outcomes described in the organization's Target Profiles (see the next section) rather than a progression from Tier 1 to Tier 4.

The final Framework document describes the implementation tiers in more detail, but the following is a summary of the four tiers, modified from NIST's description (Figure 0.4):

- **Tier 1: Partial** – Risk is managed in an ad hoc and sometimes reactive manner. There is limited awareness of cybersecurity risk at the organizational level with no organization-wide approach to cybersecurity.

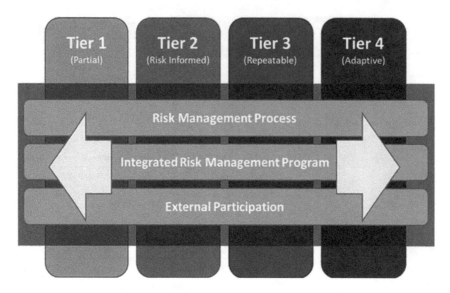

FIGURE 0.4 NIST Implementation Tiers.

The organization may not have the processes in place to participate in coordination or collaboration with other entities.

- **Tier 2: Risk-Informed** – Management approves risk management practices, but they may not be an organization-wide policy. There is awareness of cybersecurity risk at the organization level. Still, an organization-wide approach has not been established, and the organization understands the broader ecosystem but has not formalized its participation in it.
- **Tier 3: Repeatable** – The organization's risk management practices are approved and formally adopted as policy. There is an organization-wide approach to risk management. The organization collaborates with and receives information from partners in the wider ecosystem.
- **Tier 4: Adaptive** – The organization adapts its cybersecurity practices from lessons learned. Cybersecurity risk management uses risk-informed policies, procedures, and processes and is part of the organizational culture and the organization actively shares information with partners.

FRAMEWORK PROFILE

The Framework Profile is a blueprint or map that considers the Framework's functions, categories, and subcategories for a specific purpose tailored to the organization's needs. Organizations should develop profiles for current or desired cybersecurity objectives, and some organizations can create multiple profiles for different segments or aspects of the organization.

No template for what a profile should look like exists because Framework users should tailor their profiles to their organizations' specific needs. As NIST points out, there is no right or wrong way to develop a profile. As Figure 0.5 illustrates, the factors that could go into a profile are an organization's business

FIGURE 0.5 NIST Framework Risk Management Cycle.

objectives, threat environment, requirements, and controls, all of which create a cybersecurity profile unique to that organization.

The profiles' vital aspect compares where an organization is currently and where an organization wishes to be – its target. As NIST states in the Framework document, "this risk-based approach enables an organization to gauge resource estimates (e.g. staffing, funding) to achieve cybersecurity goals in a cost-effective, prioritized manner."[7]

OTHER ASPECTS OF THE FRAMEWORK DOCUMENT

Although the Core, Tiers, and Profiles are the most critical parts of the Framework, the document released in February 2014 and updated in 2018 also contains other useful pieces of information, including tips on using the Framework and advice on communicating the importance of the Framework to stakeholders.

RECENT DEVELOPMENTS AT NIST

In response to a series of damaging and high-profile cyberattacks involving Chinese state-sponsored threat actors and Russian ransomware operators, President Joe Biden released a wide-ranging and ambitious executive order (EO) on May 12, 2021, the *President's Executive Order (EO) on "Improving the Nation's Cybersecurity (14028)*. The EO assigns NIST several complex tasks that reshape U.S. cybersecurity policy and requirements. They also elevate the

---

[7]NIST Framework p. 11.

foundational importance of the NIST cybersecurity framework's core functions of identifying, protecting, detecting, responding, and recovering. (See https://www.nist.gov/itl/executive-order-improving-nations-cybersecurity).

As of this book's publication date, many of these NIST mandates are still in process. In addition, it's important to note that any requirements coming out of the EO apply only to federal government agencies and their contractors. But, under the theory that most of the world's leading tech companies are also major suppliers to the federal government, it's likely that the EO and the NIST requirements would ultimately have spill-over effects for private sector organizations.

The NIST assignments in the EO include:

- **Developing guidance to help agencies achieve "zero-trust" architecture.** Zero-trust is the latest trend in cybersecurity that "eliminates implicit trust in any one element, node, or service and instead requires continuous verification of the operational picture via real-time information from multiple sources to determine access and other system responses," according to the EO.
- **Defining what constitutes "critical software" and publishing guidance outlining security measures for critical software.** These intricate tasks aim to prevent the infiltration of malware into widely used and essential software.
- **Developing guidelines that result in minimum standards for vendors' testing of their software source code.** These guidelines aim to put into place processes to ensure that software is sufficiently safe and secure.
- **Publishing guidance that identifies practices to enhance software supply chain security.** This guidance aims to foreclose, to the extent feasible, malicious software from third parties from sneaking into the various subcomponents that make up modern software.
- **Initiating labeling programs related to the Internet of Things (IoT) and software to inform consumers about the security of their products.** This task aims to provide consumers with a ratings scale that helps them better understand the security level of their hardware IoT devices and software.

The Cybersecurity Framework is a critical reference document for organizations to consult in the NIST tasks completed or underway. In particular, all the software security measures count the Framework as an informative reference.

CHAPTER 1

Cybersecurity Risk Planning and Management

Overview of Chapter and Objective

This chapter is the most foundational section of the book because it discusses how to establish knowledge of the systems in place and how to inform management of those systems' risk profiles. It also discusses how to develop plans for dealing with the highest priority risks. The goal is to help the reader develop an understanding necessary to manage cybersecurity risk to systems, assets, data, and capabilities.

Johnson Transportation is one of the world's largest shipping companies. Joanna, the director of network management inside the company's IT department, is walking toward the office kitchen to get a cup of afternoon coffee when she passes a colleague's office.

Out of the corner of her eye, she sees that the screen on his desk suddenly goes dark.

As she walks past another colleague's desk, another screen goes dark. She keeps walking and sees that screens are blacking out as far as she can see. She wonders if there has been a power failure in the server room, which has twice shut down systems suddenly. She heads back to her desk.

Her phone is ringing, and a junior IT engineer is sitting in her office. She has a growing sense of dread that something is really, fundamentally wrong. Tom, the company's CIO, calls her to ask if she has any information on the computer blackouts. Joanna tells him she has no idea what happened or where the problem originated.

Cybersecurity Risk Management: Mastering the Fundamentals Using the NIST Cybersecurity Framework, First Edition. Cynthia Brumfield and Brian Haugli.
© 2022 Cynthia Brumfield and Brian Haugli. Published 2022 by John Wiley & Sons, Inc.

She checks with John, the head of IT, who is as mystified as she is about the blackout. Some systems, such as voice communications, shipping management, and personnel, never fully went down. They flickered briefly but are now operating normally. Something seems to be wrong with only some routers, although it's tough to tell which ones.

Joanna is now frantic. Which routers are causing the problem, and where are they? Now that she thinks of it, an IT consultant installed new routers last week. Could they be the cause of the problem? Joanna digs through her inbox to find the consultant's paperwork on those installations. Everything has been so crazy she hasn't had time to focus on the new equipment. As her phone lines continue to ring, people are pouring into her office, wanting answers.

She calls everyone who might know what happened. After 45 minutes, she's no closer to figuring out where the possibly faulty routers are or even if they're the cause of the problem. Suddenly the company CEO, Nils, is at her office door. What's going on? All the booking systems are down – in the shipping business, booking systems control everything – and he wants to know what's going on. He asks her: "Could this be a cyberattack?"

INTRODUCTION

As Joanna's nightmare illustrates, digital security emergencies can encompass entire organizations and destroy customer relationships. If Joanna is well-prepared to manage risks, she can handle this urgent scenario so that Johnson Shipping incurs as little damage as possible.

Cybersecurity risk planning and management is the first step toward helping your enterprise follow a path toward digital security and safety. Still, it can sometimes look daunting to non-cybersecurity professionals. Just know that the first step toward managing a cyber incident is to plan for it in advance.

This book will walk you through how to establish helpful knowledge of information technology and operational technology systems you have in place and develop plans for dealing with the highest priority risks. If you follow the practical advice outlined here, you should have the necessary knowledge to begin managing cybersecurity risks to your organization's systems, assets, data, and capabilities.

I. WHAT IS CYBERSECURITY RISK MANAGEMENT?

One of the critical foundations of a secure organization is to develop a solid practice of cybersecurity risk management. What is cybersecurity risk management?

Cybersecurity risk management is simply looking at what could go wrong and then coming up with ways to minimize those problems. It's basically what most of us try to do daily to ensure things go as smoothly as possible in our lives, whether organizing our time, managing our finances, or watching over our children's lives.

In the same way, cybersecurity risk management is coming up with ways to make sure things go as smoothly as possible with our IT- and OT-related and mission-specific assets. As is true with our everyday lives, managing cybersecurity risks is an ongoing, multi-dimensional process.

One significant distinction exists with cybersecurity that doesn't always apply in our daily lives: within an organization, everyone needs to be involved in managing cybersecurity risks, from the top level of decision-makers down to the employees responsible for putting into practice the policies that decision-makers establish.

As is true in our day-to-day lives, risk management in cybersecurity can be complicated and daunting, with endless topics to explore. But what we'll cover in this chapter hits some fundamental practices and activities that should hold you in good stead as your steer your organization on the road to sound and effective cybersecurity.

A.   Risk Management Is a Process

Before we jump into actual risk planning and management practices, a bit of the necessary background is in order. In addition to the cybersecurity framework discussed in the Preface, the National Institute of Standards and Technology (NIST) has also developed a cybersecurity risk management framework that characterizes the concept as a comprehensive process that requires organizations to:

1. **Frame risk** – Determine how much risk your organization is willing to take on given constraints and upper management goals.
2. **Assess risk** – Determine the importance of various assets, know which are protected, and the degree to which the assets are vulnerable.
3. **Respond to Risk Once Determined** – Come up with plans of action if the risks turn into adverse realities.
4. **Monitor Risk on an Ongoing Basis** – Check risk plans to ensure you have implemented them and updated them as situations change based on ongoing or periodic monitoring of those plans.

Even though cybersecurity risk management should be a part of everybody's job in an organization, it's crucial to establish clear roles of responsibility within your organization of who will be held accountable for the risks you face or who will "own" the risks you face, as we discuss later in the chapter. Although this job has typically fallen on the organization's chief information security officer (CISO) or comparable IT executive, some cybersecurity experts are increasingly recommending that the ownership of risk should fall on the executives who have to cover costs if the threat materializes.

This notion of assigning ownership based on materialized risk losses may not fit your organization or business model. But the point is to establish clarity of risk responsibility and roles throughout your organization. Otherwise, some or even many risks may fall through the cracks of diffused responsibility, and you may never address them adequately until it's too late.

The next section will walk you through some of these components of cybersecurity risk management. Specifically, we will introduce you to key concepts in the NIST cybersecurity framework, as discussed in the Preface.

II. ASSET MANAGEMENT

When it comes to asset management, most people first think about a crucial cybersecurity element, commonly called "security hygiene." On a day-to-day basis, all IT and OT assets must be appropriately managed and kept in as secure a manner as possible.

Among the top tasks in this practice of good cybersecurity hygiene, you should:

- patch software as soon as vendor security updates are issued, unless your patch management approach suggests otherwise,
- protect all relevant systems with up-to-date antivirus protection, and
- secure all assets through access controls, including authentication (strong passwords, multi-factor for critical systems externally accessible) and authorization (role-based access control or least privilege).

Fundamentally, at the core of any cybersecurity risk assessment or management program is knowing what assets you have, keeping track of them, and making sure you know which assets employees, vendors, and others have permission to use. In the NIST Framework's parlance, most functions that qualify as asset management fall under the core function of "Identify."

All asset management efforts first require identifying those assets to lay a foundation for managing risks to those assets. It is almost impossible to protect systems and software – and your organization – without first developing a process to identify those systems and software.

Voices of Experience
On Asset Management

If you don't know what you have, you don't know what you need to protect

The most fundamental thing that organizations should be doing is asset management. If you don't know what you have, you don't know what you need to protect or how to protect it or what change management looks like or what a supply chain looks like. There are so many things that stem from simply knowing and managing what you have.

Most business don't want to spend the time, money, or effort to manage their assets that way. If I manage my most critical stuff at least kind of well, I'm probably doing enough to not hemorrhage money or go out of business.

The key challenge for them is to understand what's critical.

I work with a lot of boards and executives. It's basically their jobs to take as much risk as they can. It's not to take as little risk as they can. In fact, it's exactly the opposite. So, you're looking at the leadership of the organization, in almost every case is driving as fast and as hard as they can to take as much risk as they possibly can. The risk management side of the house is looking at it from exactly the opposite perspective.

Patrick Miller, founder of the Energy Sector Security Consortium and U.S. Coordinator for the Industrial Cybersecurity Center

The NIST Framework defines the outcome or goal of asset management as the "data, personnel, devices, systems, and facilities that enable the organization to achieve business purposes are identified and managed consistent with their relative importance to business objectives and the organization's risk strategy."

The set of processes that make up asset management are designed to manage the life cycle and inventory of technology assets providing value to organizations by:

- lowering IT and OT costs,
- reducing IT and OT risk,
- improving productivity through proper and predefined asset management,
- maximizing the value of the organization's assets, and
- increasing knowledge of who in the organization needs what kinds of assets.

In this section, we'll review some of the critical aspects of asset management that you should know to keep your operations as secure and reliable as possible.

A.   Inventory Every Physical Device and System You Have and Keep the Inventory Updated

This recommendation closely aligns with a critical subcategory of the NIST Framework, which is "ID.AM-1: Physical devices and systems within the organization are inventoried." We recommend you learn more about this subcategory and all the NIST subcategories we reference throughout the book.

We'll provide some helpful technical standard and informative reference resources at the end of each section that NIST has mapped to its Framework.

One of the most important and yet least practiced cybersecurity tasks conducted worldwide is to conduct asset inventories and keep them updated. You cannot defend what you don't know exists.

This critical task should extend to your headquarters or remote locations, whether that's a local Starbucks or a home office in Kansas City. You can create an up-to-date inventory of all assets that store or process information on a simple spreadsheet for smaller organizations or within a configuration management database (CMDB) for large organizations. The critical requirement is that an inventory is kept and maintained. Many organizations fail on this crucial security activity because they do not know where to start.

One straightforward approach is to gather your team to just whiteboard a list of systems types. For example:

End-user device

- laptops
- phones

Servers

- virtual
- physical

Cloud platform

- SaaS
- PaaS
- IaaS

Voices of Experience
On Asset Management

Work from Home Environments Raise the Stakes on Asset Management

One of the things that we did as we established a single source of truth is we combined the asset management details with the HR records and what were one of the things that we started watching for was if people were shipping back their laptops shortly after they're no longer with the company. That's something that we wanted to automate because we're such a distributed workforce in the post pandemic work from home kind of environment. You know you don't want to have something that requires them to go physically to IT and IT to manually record the status. You want to put the data to work. So this asset management data can be combined with HR datasets to provide visibility into our people following important processes around decommissioning assets as well.

Omer Singer, Head of Cyber Security Strategy, Snowflake

This starting point will be the basis to determine where to keep the inventory going forward. If it's a short list for a small company, an Excel or Google sheet will suffice.

Updates to the inventory can come from various internal sources, such as when procurement or IT requests and purchases new equipment, such as laptops or servers. Relevant personnel can send simple e-mails notifying the responsible party of the addition.

For more mature operations, submitting a ticketing system or, even better, automatically creating the configuration management database (CMDB) asset are good options. Make sure to include with relevant records the necessary data to identify it, such as its network address, hardware address, machine name, data asset owner, and department for each asset and whether the right personnel approved the asset's connection to the network. Where possible, you should tie the software inventory into the hardware asset inventory so that you can track all devices and associated software from a single location.

Inventories must extend to include cloud components, software as a service (SaaS), platform as a service (PaaS), and infrastructure as service (IaaS). For SaaS specifically, this should include e-mail and web hosting solutions and HR platforms, marketing tools, legal platforms, and file repositories.

Adding and updating the inventory must also include removing unauthorized assets from the network. This process can entail physically removing systems or quarantining them via software methods to restrict their ability to communicate on the internet. Many current endpoint detection and response (EDR) solutions and some antivirus solutions provide this capability.

Inventorying every physical device and system you have means:

- actively managing all hardware devices on the network so that you give only authorized devices access, and
- finding unauthorized and unmanaged devices and preventing them from gaining access to your networks.

This inventory should include, at a minimum, all devices that have an IP address. But it should also include all assets with the potential to store or process information, including assets that you do not connect to a network. All these devices could be potential entry points for an attacker. Any weak link in the IT or OT chain can lead to further system vulnerabilities or even complete system compromise and takeover by hackers and attackers.

Among the traditional IT devices that you should include in this inventory are:

- desktops,
- laptops,
- mobile devices (you should segment employee devices – BYODs or "bring your own devices" – that connect or can connect to your networks),
- printers,
- databases,
- Windows and UNIX/Linux servers,
- backup systems,
- removable storage media, including USB devices,
- voice-over-IP telephone systems,
- storage area networks, and
- network equipment such as routers, switches, and firewall software.

As new Internet-of-Things (IoT) devices enter the home and workplace, your inventory should also consider these potential entry points into your system. Among the types of IP-connected devices that bad actors can quickly turn into attack vectors are:

- Voice-activated digital assistants such as Siri, Cortana, Google, or Alexa.
- Internet-connected industrial building systems such as HVAC systems, lighting systems, and so forth.
- Internet-connected appliances such as Wi-Fi-connected kitchen machines, including coffee makers, refrigerators, and ovens.

All organizations need to pay attention to traditional and emerging IT hardware assets and an extensive list of IoT devices and specialized equipment your organization uses. Although not all digital equipment is designed for connectivity to the internet, increasingly, many types of equipment, particularly newer models of gear, come with IP addresses or at least the potential for internet connectivity.

You'll see in Figure 1.1 the types of equipment that you should consider including in your inventory in addition to the traditional IT assets. The items in this table are by no means exhaustive.

Hardware Assets to Include in Asset Inventory

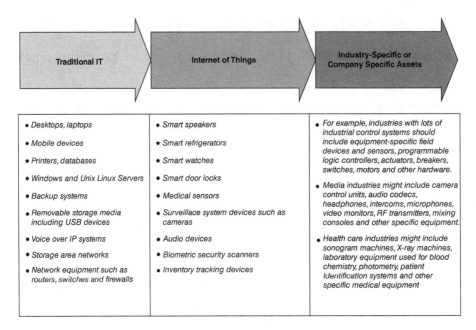

Traditional IT	Internet of Things	Industry-Specific or Company Specific Assets
• Desktops, laptops	• Smart speakers	• For example, industries with lots of industrial control systems should include equipment-specific field devices and sensors, programmable logic controllers, actuators, breakers, switches, motors and other hardware.
• Mobile devices	• Smart refrigerators	
• Printers, databases	• Smart watches	
• Windows and Unix Linux Servers	• Smart door locks	
• Backup systems	• Medical sensors	• Media industries might include camera control units, audio codecs, headphones, intercoms, microphones, video monitors, RF transmitters, mixing consoles and other specific equipment.
• Removable storage media including USB devices	• Surveillace system devices such as cameras	
• Voice over IP systems	• Audio devices	• Health care industries might include sonogram machines, X-ray machines, laboratory equipment used for blood chemistry, photometry, patient Identification systems and other specific medical equipment
• Storage area networks	• Biometric security scanners	
• Network equipment such as routers, switches and firewalls	• Inventory tracking devices	

FIGURE 1.1   Hardware Assets.

Your organization may have greater or fewer types of equipment to include in your inventory. A dynamic host configuration protocol (DHCP) logging on all DHCP servers or IP address management tools can help update the organization's hardware asset inventory.

Once you conduct the inventory, your job is not done. The inventory should be updated frequently to ensure accuracy. It is helpful to use an active discovery tool to identify devices connected to the organization's network and update the hardware asset inventory.

Finally, all the inventory work can be made more accessible by a network monitoring system that alerts administrators to the presence on the network of unauthorized devices. These systems can scan the network and monitor systems on a 24/7 basis or at periodic intervals, looking for authorized and unauthorized devices and alert administrators to the network's presence of unknown devices.

Many of these monitoring systems are free, but commercially available systems are options to consider. Without such network monitoring, employees can attach unauthorized devices to the network, defeating the purpose of developing the inventory in the first place.

You should conduct regular testing of the network monitoring system to see if the system catches all new hardware (or software, as we discuss in the next section) you add. You should remove or quarantine unauthorized assets until you update the inventory in a timely manner.

A helpful method for identifying unauthorized assets is to ensure that the hardware asset inventory records the network address, hardware address, machine name, data asset owner, and department for each asset and note whether the assets are connected to the internet.

The following are some specific technical standards that might help IT specialists delve deeper into the subject of physical device inventory management:

Relevant Technical Standards for ID.AM-1

- CCS CSC 1
- COBIT 5 BAI09.01, BAI09.02
- ISA 62443-2-1:2009 4.2.3.4
- ISA 62443-3-3:2013 SR 7.8
- ISO/IEC 27001:2013 A.8.1.1, A.8.1.2
- NIST SP 800-53 Rev. 4 CM-8

B. Inventory Every Software Platform and Application You Use and Keep the Inventory Updated

The NIST Framework subcategory that covers this aspect of cyber risk management is known as "ID.AM-2: Software platforms and applications within the organization are inventoried."

Much like the concept of inventorying every physical device in the organization, creating a software inventory is crucial to:

- actively tracking all software on the network so that only authorized software is installed and can execute and
- helping to ensure unauthorized and unmanaged software is found and prevented from installation or execution.

Most organizations find that creating an inventory for software is more complicated than doing so for hardware. A wider variety of software is used, and trusted employees frequently download software. Still, software inventories should track all software used on general IT hardware such as:

- desktops,
- servers,
- workstations,
- laptops, and
- mobile devices owned by the organization.

In drawing up the software inventory, take a holistic view of your organization's operations and functions to develop as comprehensive a list as possible for the software used in each chain of operations.

As is also true of hardware inventories, using an automated software inventory tracking tool can make the process far more comfortable and practical. This software tracking tool:

- can also be used to help pinpoint the installation of unauthorized or potentially unsafe software installed by employees,
- can help keep track of the software patches that most software suppliers issue on an ongoing basis, and

■ can also help administrators implement white lists of software, barring employee installation of any software not on the white lists.

Just as is the case for hardware inventories, you should update software inventories regularly.

A good scenario would be to implement a combination of endpoint management and control by whitelisting or blacklisting software applications. End users will want the ability to access productivity tools, creating a central clearinghouse of software, either by an approved software depot (maybe a file share or website) or by a platform that publishes approved software that auto deploys for installation.

The software should be reviewed, tested (if possible), and approved before deployment to the repo (data repository) or, at the very least, installation. Ideally, each package deployed is currently supported by the vendor, or it's tagged as unsupported. Unsupported software should find its way onto a deprecation list to sunset so the organization cannot carry technical "debt." Also, tagging unsupported software helps with patching or vulnerability management, which we'll get to in later subcategories.

If you're tracking cloud applications, specifically SaaS, in an inventory aligned to ID.AM-1, there is no need to double count those applications in your software inventory.

You can build software inventories while meeting other security requirements. Implementation of endpoint detection and response (EDR) or some antivirus solutions should give you visibility into installed software across those covered assets. Running vulnerability management or scanning platforms should provide you with visibility into software installed in each scanned system. These systems can be combined or used by themselves to start gathering the deployed or installed software in your environment.

An ideal solution would be a single inventory with physical or virtual devices. You should record each software component installed on each device with the corresponding name, version number, install date, and current support status from the vendor.

The following technical standards list is worth exploring for learners who want to dig deeper into conducting and managing software inventories.

Relevant Technical Standards for ID.AM-2

- CCS CSC 2
- COBIT 5 BAI09.01, BAI09.02, BAI09.05
- ISA 62443-2-1:2009 4.2.3.4
- ISA 62443-3-3:2013 SR 7.8
- ISO/IEC 27001:2013 A.8.1.1, A.8.1.2

C. Prioritize Every Device, Software Platform, and Application Based on Importance

This risk planning component entails developing criteria and assigning a priority rating to manage each logical control system's risk. It is encompassed in the NIST subcategory of "ID.AM-5: Resources (e.g., hardware, devices, data, and software) are prioritized based on their classification, criticality, and business value."

This prioritization means establishing formal access control used to assign a security level to an asset and determine which people can use it. You can devise any classification system to determine the priority levels that best suits your organization, and it doesn't have to be tricky. Still, it does have to be specific enough to determine priority levels and achieve a ranking of importance. It can be as simple as "internal, external, and highly sensitive." You should assign each asset to only one category, so make sure the categories are mutually exclusive.

This process of developing criteria for asset importance can be a conversation starter within the organization to draw out what is vital to the organization. Having a classification framework can engage people to explain what is essential to their work.

This process of engaging people to explain what is essential can help develop the prioritization scheme. A problematic component of this step is deciding which assets have the most business value. Many factors can come into play in determining where in the ranking any asset might fall.

Some factors to take into account when developing priority ratings might be:

- the role the asset plays in generating revenue,
- the degree of how integral the asset is to ongoing operations,
- how frequently bad actors target the asset for exploitation,
- how expensive the asset is to replace,
- how expensive the asset is to protect, and
- the reputational or legal damage that would ensue if the asset were compromised.

These factors are merely suggestions. You need to develop your priority list based on your unique circumstances and document how you created the priorities. The critical point is that you develop standard criteria for identifying the mission criticality of all assets.

When prioritizing assets, one thing to keep in mind is maintaining an inventory of all sensitive information stored, processed, or transmitted by the organization's technology systems, including those located on site or at a remote service provider.

For more detailed technical help in this prioritization, the following standards and resources could be helpful:

Relevant Technical Standards for ID.RA-5

- COBIT 5 APO12.02
- ISO/IEC 27001:2013 A.12.6.1
- NIST SP 800-53 Rev. 4 RA-2, RA-3, PM-16

D. Establish Personnel Security Requirements Including Third-Party Stakeholders

This component of cyber risk planning and management maps to NIST's subcategory "ID.AM-6: Cybersecurity roles and responsibilities for the entire workforce and third-party stakeholders (e.g., suppliers, customers, partners) are established."

Before you get to this activity, it's advisable to create a security awareness program for all workforce members to complete regularly to ensure they understand and exhibit the necessary behaviors and skills to ensure the organization's security. You should develop the organization's security awareness program so that you communicate the central lessons engagingly.

In essence, establishing personnel security requirements means you decide which personnel at all levels, executives, management, staff, and third-party stakeholders (vendors, customers, and partners), have access to what assets, at what level of a security clearance, under what conditions. The importance of knowing who has access to various assets within your organization and outside your organization will only increase as the number of devices used and platforms over which content gets delivered grow. Without user-defined roles and responsibilities, the ability to maintain security across all surfaces is substantially weakened, particularly in times of system breaches and malfunctions.

Some essential tasks to undertake in defining workforce and third-party roles are:

- requiring third-party providers to comply with personnel security policies and procedures established by the organization,
- documenting personnel security requirements,
- defining minimum acceptable standards of information security requirements that you should include in all contracts (and adding addenda or exhibits for exceptional cases such as PCI – payment card industry – conditions), and
- establishing a right to audit clauses within contracts or through a third-party attestation.

Although establishing security requirements for organizational personnel is a relatively routine activity (e.g., few people within any organization have full admin privileges to critical systems), establishing those requirements for third-party providers can be challenging. Third-party providers are sometimes hard to identify and even more difficult to track regarding their personnel changes and security requirements.

Outside contractors, including IT support personnel, software developers, website designers, vendors, system support consultants, or any other third party that routinely require access to your organization's network, should include in their agreements with your organization personnel requirements and security levels as are necessary for each person. All third parties should also be required to provide your organization with timely notification of any personnel changes as a routine matter.

The same procedures for informing employees, executives, and any other internal organizational staff of their security rights and responsibilities should also apply to third parties. This uniformity of using the same levels of information, rights, and responsibilities to both internal and external parties will help you more efficiently track and make necessary adjustments to the various levels of system security over time.

One of the crucial steps in establishing personnel security requirements is to gain buy-in from the organization's top. An executive or someone within the leadership team must set the tone that cybersecurity is part of the organization through its training, development, implementation, and culture. Beyond setting the tone, someone must be designated to lead the cybersecurity program, assess the organization's risks, map a plan to reduce those risks, and then execute that plan to reach a target state.

Whether your organization is small or large, you should designate personnel by role and name by their cybersecurity responsibilities. This designation will help immensely later on when you need to establish vulnerability management and incident response capabilities.

If you have valuable vendors or critical providers to your services identified, you should integrate them into your cybersecurity program. This integration holds even if you outsource your security to a managed security service provider (MSSP) or a security operations center (SOC).

The following technical standards are helpful resources for more technical insight into how best to establish and maintain personnel security requirements:

Relevant Technical Standards for ID.AM-6

- COBIT 5 APO01.02, DSS06.03
- ISA 62443-2-1:2009 4.3.2.3.3
- ISO/IEC 27001:2013 A.6.1.1
- NIST SP 800-53 Rev. 4 CP-2, PS-7, PM-11

III. GOVERNANCE

Cyber risk planning and management's governance aspect covers the policies, procedures, and processes to manage and monitor your organization's regulatory, legal, risk, environmental, and operational requirements. It's a way of:

- defining a set of actions to protect against the threats and vulnerabilities your organization faces,
- establishing formal management policies, and
- seeing to it that they're carried out on a day-to-day basis.

A. Make Sure You Educate Management about Risks

One of the most critical aspects of governance for IT, cybersecurity, and other technical professionals to know is that you need to educate top management about cybersecurity risks so they can factor those risks into their decision-making. (This part of cyber risk planning and management aligns with the "ID.GV-4: Governance and risk management processes address cybersecurity risks" in the NIST Framework.)

As cybersecurity risks escalate, boards of directors and C-Suite executives are increasingly held responsible for managing cyber threats by shareholders and other stakeholders. In some industries, regulators are watching, which puts even more of an onus on top executives to stay informed.

So regardless of your organization's size, developing a system for informing top decision-makers of cybersecurity risks will likely play an ever-more important part in your job. Your plan need not be elaborate or formal, and top-level decision-makers don't need to become experts on technical matters. They do, however, need to understand the competitive implications of cybersecurity risk.

Once you've worked out a system for informing top management, the board of directors, or any relevant organizational committees, it's important to

---

Voices of Experience
On Governance

Know Your Laws and Regulations

The most important thing is to first understand which laws and regulations you need to comply with. That is really the baseline of what you need to know to understand and make sure that all the governance and policy structure covers your organization. It is different by industry, by size of your company, and the physical locations that you operate in. You also need to rely on your partners within the company, as you may not have all the answers. I know in my history, I have always had close relationships with both legal and HR. Coming from a life sciences background, Quality Control and E-discovery are integral partners on privacy issues to address the FDA regulations we had.

Bill Roberts, former CISO at Hologic

---

schedule regular updates for these constituents. Suppose your organization is structured in a way that these top-level updates can't easily take place. In that case, it might be worthwhile to create a cyber risk advisory council that can then provide reports or updates to the board and executive management.

One approach is to establish a dedicated information risk steering committee that validates your risk management program's strategic direction and commits to appropriate resource levels and investments for addressing cybersecurity risks.

Ideally, an executive-level steering committee composed of business, regional, and functional leaders is accountable to the board of directors for the program's success. It is responsible for providing the program leader with risk management direction. Overall, the goal should be to get cybersecurity viewed as an operational risk, not just an IT risk where leaders pass it off as merely a technical issue.

Many mom-and-pop and mid-sized organizations tend to outsource the management of cybersecurity risks. If that's your situation, and you outsource to a cybersecurity vendor, good cybersecurity governance still requires you to develop a governance framework that keeps top management plugged into your particular risk profile.

We next include some references to help you learn more about applicable technical standards that could help you develop your organizations' governance policy:

> ## Relevant Technical Standards for ID.GV-4
>
> - COBIT 5 DSS04.02
> - ISA 62443-2-1:2009 4.2.3.1, 4.2.3.3, 4.2.3.8, 4.2.3.9, 4.2.3.11, 4.3.2.4.3, 4.3.2.6.3
> - NIST SP 800-53 Rev. 4 PM-9, PM-11

IV. RISK ASSESSMENT AND MANAGEMENT

A risk assessment is simply an effort to identify threats to your organization, how likely they are, and the consequences of the dangers. It would help if you used risk assessments to support your organization's strategy, giving you the information you need to deploy specific practices and controls to address the risks you identify. They also help you assess how effective your procedures and rules for managing risks are.

Risk assessments typically precede risk management, which we will cover later. The best approach is to implement a risk assessment framework, which will help you develop objective measurements of risk and better protect at-risk assets. It would help if you used the risk assessment framework as a helpful guide for determining what is assessed, who needs to be involved, and the criteria for developing relative degrees of risk. In short, they are tools for making sense of what can be a very complex idea to implement.

Among some of the frameworks in use by other industries are:

- Operationally Critical Threat, Asset, and Vulnerability Evaluation (OCTAVE), from Carnegie Mellon University,
- NIST SP 800-30, Guide for Conducting Risk Assessments, and
- ISACA's RISK IT (part of COBIT 5), ISO/IEC 27005:2011 (part of the ISO 27000 series that includes ISO 27001 and 27002).

A. Know Where You're Vulnerable

Identifying where your organization has vulnerabilities is a fundamental first step to conducting a full risk assessment. This aspect of cyber risk planning and management falls under the NIST Framework as "ID.RA-1: Asset vulnerabilities are identified and documented."

The Council on Cybersecurity defines vulnerability assessments as an effort to "continuously acquire, assess, and take action on new information to identify vulnerabilities, remediate, and minimize the window of opportunity for attackers."[1]

Knowing where you are vulnerable is contingent on having complete and updated hardware and software inventories. You cannot identify vulnerabilities on software and assets if you don't know they exist. You can leverage automated tools and risk registers to document the risks associated with those assets.

---

[1] https://www.cisecurity.org.

Employees operating or overseeing the vulnerability management program for the organization should be trained on all the automated tools and methods to identify new vulnerabilities. They should also be responsible for the proper handling of vulnerabilities that are disclosed to the organization by third parties.

Investigating where you're vulnerable can entail many activities, including:

- using vulnerability scanning tools through your organization's systems and
- keeping abreast of vendor security alert announcements and periodic attack and penetration testing.

There is no one-size-fits-all approach for conducting vulnerability assessments because so much depends on your particular technical configuration, how large your organization is, and many other factors.

The following are some sound technical standards that might give you some ideas about implementing a sound vulnerability assessment initiative:

Relevant Technical Standards for ID.RA-1

- CCS CSC 4
- COBIT 5 APO12.01, APO12.02, APO12.03, APO12.04
- ISA 62443-2-1:2009 4.2.3, 4.2.3.7, 4.2.3.9, 4.2.3.12
- ISO/IEC 27001:2013 A.12.6.1, A.18.2.3
- NIST SP 800-53 Rev. 4 CA-2, CA-7, CA-8, RA-3, RA-5, SA-5, SA-11, SI-2, SI-4, SI-5

B.   Identify the Threats You Face, Both Internally and Externally

Once you've identified your vulnerabilities, a good next step is to identify the threats or kind of threats you most commonly face from both internal actors (e.g., disgruntled employees) and external attackers. This step in cyber risk planning and management dovetails with the NIST Framework's subcategory "ID.RA-3: Threats, both internal and external, are identified and documented."

A useful definitional distinction between assessing vulnerabilities and identifying threats could be helpful. Vulnerabilities are those aspects of your systems that attackers can exploit. Threats are the tools that attackers use to exploit those vulnerabilities.

It's entirely possible to find vulnerabilities in your systems for which no threats or exploits seem to have been developed, and none seem likely on the horizon. The best means of identifying whether your vulnerabilities are targeted for exploitation and how best to deal with those vulnerabilities is to participate in established formal or informal information-sharing programs where your peers share the kind of threats they've experienced and how they have dealt with them. Participating in other cybersecurity forums and staying abreast of cybersecurity news are also means of identifying the threats you face.

Ideally, automated tools or systems should be in place to ensure that both internal and external threats are identified and eventually documented. If you can perform some fundamental threat modeling, this is a significant effort that will enhance your security posture.

Threat modeling could be as simple as taking a disgruntled employee and determining through a tabletop exercise the damage that employee could inflict on the organization. An essential step in this tabletop exercise would be to identify the vulnerable systems this employee would access. You could extend this exercise to external threats such as nation-states, if applicable, or commodity malware and other types of lower levels attacks.

The following are some technical standards that might help you delve deeper into the threat identification practices you could find helpful:

Relevant Technical Standards for ID.RA-3

- COBIT 5 APO12.01, APO12.02, APO12.03, APO12.04
- ISA 62443-2-1:2009 4.2.3, 4.2.3.9, 4.2.3.12
- NIST SP 800-53 Rev. 4 RA-3, SI-5, PM-12, PM-16

C. Focus on the Vulnerabilities and Threats That Are Most Likely AND Pose the Highest Risk to Assets

This aspect of cyber risk planning and management appears in the NIST Framework subcategory of "ID.RA-5: Threats, vulnerabilities, likelihoods, and impacts are used to determine risk." In essence, this means that once you know where you're vulnerable, the kind of threats you face, and the likelihood of those threats, focus on the vulnerabilities and threats with the highest risk to essential assets.

Some vulnerabilities will leave the organization open to more damage than other vulnerabilities, even if the likelihood of threats is low. Some threats will be minor annoyances, while others promise to shut down operations. Decide where the most significant risks to the most critical assets are and focus on those first.

For example, let's say the chief criteria you use to rank the importance of assets are whether or not the asset is crucial to maintaining your e-commerce system's reliability. Suppose your organization's content server has vulnerabilities, but exploits of those vulnerabilities are unlikely. In that case, you may still rate that asset as highly important from a risk perspective because any threat to the content server, however low, could threaten e-commerce activity.

The reverse is also true. Let's say your organization's public address system has vulnerabilities, and the threat of exploitation is very high – your colleagues who use the same network have been hit with malware that cripples the same public address system. Despite this, you might rate this asset as lower in importance, despite the greater frequency of possible attack, because your chief goals are to maintain your e-commerce system, and your internal public address system outage won't affect that system.

Using the criteria you developed for your assets' importance, the next step is to determine your risk levels by factoring how likely those assets are to be successfully targeted.

Figure 1.2 might give you a sense of the risk prioritization involved in this step. As you can see, the level of threats and the value of the assets, however determined, can intersect in all kinds of ways to create high or low risks. It's all a matter of how you score your assets and how you assess the likelihood of threats.

Some organizations may be willing to accept risks in some circumstances because the cost of addressing those risks may outweigh the foreseeable harm. These risks are referred to as residual risks but are tracked in the risk assessment process like higher-level risks.

For organizations short on time and personnel, several different methods determine your risk level for various assets. The simplest is using an excel spreadsheet to document the vulnerabilities and the likelihood and the potential impact that a known risk could have on a system or the organization.

Some useful tasks that should be helpful in risk prioritization are:

- using vulnerability scanning tools through your organization's systems and
- keeping abreast of vendor security alert announcements and periodic attack and penetration testing.

The following technical standards could help develop this kind of risk determination:

Relevant Technical Standards for ID.RA-5

- COBIT 5 APO12.02
- ISO/IEC 27001:2013 A.12.6.1
- NIST SP 800-53 Rev. 4 RA-2, RA-3, PM-16

D.   Develop Plans for Dealing with the Highest Risks

This final component of this chapter deals with efforts addressed in the NIST Framework subcategory "ID.RA-6: Risk responses are identified and prioritized" as well as "ID.RM-1: Risk management processes are established, managed, and agreed to by organizational stakeholders."

Coming up with plans for dealing with the highest risks means figuring out what likely response you will have to the highest risk threats and coming up with some strategic options and actions for addressing those risks. Any response plans you have should be consistent with your organization's goals (e.g., while implementing malware removal, you can't just shut down access to e-commerce systems entirely, but you might be able to shut down other nonessential systems, such as invoice processing).

NIST lays out the process for dealing with the highest risks, saying that the organization should:

1. Implement a process for ensuring that plans of action and milestones for the security program and associated organizational information systems:

Asset Value and Threat Likelihood to Determine Risk Level

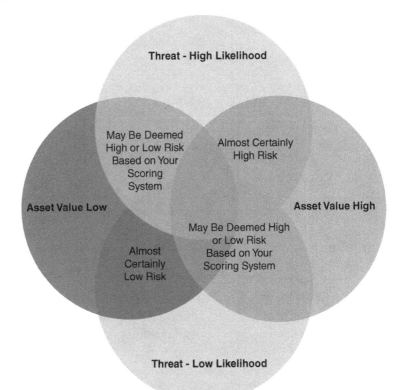

FIGURE 1.2 Determining Threat Likelihood.

    a. are developed and maintained and

    b. document the remedial information security actions to adequately respond to risk to organizational operations and assets, individuals, other organizations, and the nation.

  2. Review plans of action and milestones for consistency with the organizational risk management strategy and organization-wide priorities for risk response actions.

This process requires that each option or action has an "owner" within the organization responsible for the activity, although a manager can delegate authority to subordinates, where appropriate. More importantly, this aspect of risk management should be viewed from an organizational perspective and highlights the need to bring in all stakeholders across the organization when developing response plans.

    These assessments can take the form of scenario-testing, where hypothetical threats and risks are modeled on a role-playing or drill basis. Such scenario-testing or assessments can give an organization comfort that when real-world cybersecurity threats arise, the cyber risk planning and management efforts that you've undertaken have paid off in increased security and peace of mind.

It would help if you integrated information risk processes into day-to-day activities, like launching new products or services or adapting to a change in regulation or acquisition or other significant events. You can find further resources on this component of cyber risk planning and management in the following technical standards:

Relevant Technical Standards for ID.RA-6

- COBIT 5 APO12.05, APO13.02
- NIST SP 800-53 Rev. 4 PM-4, PM-9

SUMMARY

We've covered quite a bit of ground in this chapter. To recap, here are some of the highlights of cyber risk planning and management you've learned:

- Cyber risk planning and management are learning what can go wrong and the steps you can take to minimize the problems that might occur.
- The NIST Framework for Improving Critical Infrastructure Cybersecurity is a useful resource for developing your cyber risk planning and management strategies.
- Asset management can help you know what assets you have, keep track of them, and make sure you know which assets employees, vendors, and others have permission to use, all good foundations for cybersecurity risk planning and management.
- Hardware and software inventories are critical for prioritizing risk.
- Prioritizing risk requires developing a system for ranking the importance of organizational assets.
- Personnel at all levels, including third-party stakeholders, should be assigned to their access levels. Those levels determine who has access to what assets, at what level of security clearance, and under what conditions.
- Your organization's top cybersecurity focus should be on those assets that are most important and face the highest risks.
- You should develop plans for the highest risks to the most critical assets, which you should coordinate and periodically test, with necessary internal and external personnel across the organization.

CHAPTER QUIZ

You might find the following short quiz fun to test your knowledge of risk management so far. You can find the correct answers at the end of the book.

1. **When it comes to planning for how you will deal with cybersecurity risks, what are the first steps your organization should take? (Select One)**
   a. Form a working group across the organization's various departments (business, technical, legal, sales) to develop a plan.

    b. Make a list of the vulnerabilities we know we have and start building our plan to address those vulnerabilities.

    c. Conduct an inventory of all our hardware and software assets.

2. **Which of the following devices should you include in your asset inventory? (Select all that apply.)**

    a. Desktops, laptops, and servers.

    b. Mobile devices owned by the organization.

    c. Equipment specific to my organization connected to the internet or capable of being connected to the internet.

    d. All of the above.

3. **How should you deal with outside IT or tech vendors or other third parties regarding access to your networks? (Select one)**

    a. I make sure that all third parties who have access to my networks comply with personnel security policies and procedures with which my own organization's employees must comply.

    b. Because the vendor is a leader in its field and many of my peers have recommended it, its cybersecurity policies are adequate to protect my organization.

    c. I limit access to my networks to only those IT or tech vendors I know well and have trusted in the past.

4. **When briefing management and decision-makers on the cyber-security risks your organization faces, which of the following is the best approach? (Select one)**

    a. Explain the risk planning and management processes we've developed in detail to inform these decision-makers fully.

    b. Cut to the bottom-line to keep everything simple.

    c. Give them enough information to understand the competitive importance of cybersecurity risks and incorporate that understanding into business planning efforts.

5. **Which of the following is the best method for determining which assets rank highest in risk priority? (Select One)**

    a. Figure out where my organization is most vulnerable and rate those assets as the highest risk.

    b. Figure out which assets get breached or attacked most and rate those assets as the highest risk.

    c. Figure out the highest risk to important assets by factoring in those assets' vulnerabilities and the degree of threats they face.

6. **Once you've figured out your highest priority risks, what is the best step toward managing those risks? (Select One)**

    a. Develop a response plan to adequately deal with the risks and make sure I inform top management of this plan.

    b. Form a group of internal and external key players across the organization to help formulate a response plan and then perform regular assessments of the plan after it has been developed.

    c. Hire an outside cybersecurity firm to come up with a plan and help manage the risks.

ESSENTIAL READING ON CYBERSECURITY RISK MANAGEMENT

1. NIST, SP 800-30 Rev. 1, *Guide for Conducting Risk Assessments*, September 2012 at https://csrc.nist.gov/publications/detail/sp/800-30/rev-1/final

2. Ken Sigler and James L. Rainey, III, *Securing an IT Organization through Governance, Risk Management, and Audit (Internal Audit and IT Audit)* Taylor & Francis, 2016).

3. Nicole M. Radziwill and Morgan C. Benton, Cybersecurity Cost of Quality: Managing the Costs of Cybersecurity Risk Management, *Software Quality Professional*, Vol. 19, No. 3, September (2017), arXiv:1707.02653 [cs.CR], https://arxiv.org/abs/1707.02653.

4. Alexander A. Ganin, Phuoc Quach, Mahesh Panwar, Zachary A. Collier, Jeffrey M. Keisler, Dayton Marchese, and Igor Linkov, Multicriteria Decision Framework for Cybersecurity Risk Assessment and Management, *Risk Analysis*, September 5, 2017, https://onlinelibrary.wiley.com/doi/abs/10.1111/risa.12891.

5. Halima Ibrahim Kure and Shareeful Islam, Assets Focus Risk Management Framework for Critical Infrastructure Cybersecurity Risk Management, *IET Cyber-Physical Systems Theory and Applications*, June 3, 2019, https://ietresearch.onlinelibrary.wiley.com/doi/10.1049/iet-cps.2018.5079.

CHAPTER **2**

User and Network Infrastructure Planning and Management

Overview of Chapter and Objective

This chapter provides readers with a series of steps and tools to improve their organizations' network infrastructure protection through improved asset access control, awareness and training, data security, protection policies, maintenance procedures, and automated protection processes.

Alan, the senior IT engineer for Major Motors, Inc., is spending a relaxing Thursday night at home playing his favorite video game. His company's TeamTalk remote collaboration tool pops up in his screen's right-hand corner during the gaming session. That's weird, he thinks. He had used TeamTalk earlier in the day while working remotely from home. He had used the tool to discuss with his team how they would integrate the networks of the company's biggest acquisition to date, its former chief parts supplier Acme Motor Manufacturing.

But the meeting ended hours ago. Alan looks at the TeamTalk tool, and no one is there in the meeting room. Maybe he accidentally clicked the TeamTalk icon, he tells himself, and closes the TeamTalk window to return to his game.

When he shows up at the office the following day, everything is in chaos. The company's manufacturing system has been hacked, and the attackers are systematically erasing the firmware for some assembly line servers. Everyone is running around trying to figure out what to do.

It takes the company all day to recover from what was a sophisticated, baffling attack. Recovering from the attack wasn't easy because one of the first

Cybersecurity Risk Management: Mastering the Fundamentals Using the NIST Cybersecurity Framework, First Edition. Cynthia Brumfield and Brian Haugli.
© 2022 Cynthia Brumfield and Brian Haugli. Published 2022 by John Wiley & Sons, Inc.

things the attackers did was erase specific critical backup files. The damage caused by the unknown attackers might have been even worse had not a quick-thinking engineer cut off the power supply to critical servers, which kept damaging malware from propagating across systems.

The FBI and the forensics experts hired by Major Motors spend weeks figuring out what happened. As best they can piece together, a user account with super-user privileges to gain access to every system at the company had logged in and systematically begun scoping out assets before destroying the backup files and erasing the firmware.

However, the investigators can account for all the super-users' actions, and the log files don't show any of them logging into the systems. When the investigators tell the company's chief information security officer Jack about this, he suddenly remembers: Alan had been given temporary super-user privileges for a day to test a few potential new applications a vendor recommended. Alan wasn't on the latest list of super-users. But that had been weeks ago.

Under questioning by the investigators, Alan swears he did not log into any of the relevant systems at the time of the attacks. Investigators examine Alan's home computer and find keylogging software that captured Alan's login credentials for the TeamTalk tool. They are the same credentials Alan used for his temporary super-user access.

The investigators' report concludes that Alan's home computer was the conduit through which the attackers gained complete system authorization credentials at the company to wreak havoc.

I.   INTRODUCTION

As Alan's situation illustrates, keeping close track of user access to organizational networks can mean the difference between a secure network and a cybersecurity crisis that can subsume your organization. Building safeguards into how you plan and manage your organization's infrastructure is crucial to ongoing operations and resiliency in the face of a cyberattack. This chapter on User and Network Infrastructure Planning and Management builds on the risk assessment skills developed during the first chapter and delves into the details of how to create and implement security safeguards to protect your organization's data, systems, assets, and functions. By the end of the chapter, you will know the basic principles of evaluating risks and properly implementing solutions such as patch management, firewalls, back-ups, security awareness, awareness training, and more.

II.   INFRASTRUCTURE PLANNING AND MANAGEMENT IS ALL ABOUT PROTECTION, WHERE THE RUBBER MEETS THE ROAD

Infrastructure planning and management is all about building safeguards and security controls into your organization's networks and assets. It's all about protection. This section will rely heavily on the critical concepts in the Framework for Improving Critical Infrastructure Cybersecurity, developed by NIST, as outlined in Chapter 1.

NIST developed the Framework to help organizations of all kinds strengthen their cybersecurity practices and, in circumstances where companies are new to cybersecurity, develop and implement those practices. One of the NIST Framework's most significant components is a series of outcomes or desired secure states that fall under a "Protect" function.

This Protect function:

- supports the ability to reduce the attack surface and limit the impact of an adverse cyber event and
- entails developing and implementing the safeguards needed to minimize risk to critical assets and sensitive information, including access control, patch management, firewalls, back-ups, security awareness, and training.

According to the NIST Framework, protecting your organization involves the following six major cybersecurity categories:

- Access Control
- Awareness and Training
- Data Security
- Information Protection Processes and Procedures
- Maintenance
- Protective Technology

We'll walk you through each of these essential protection activities in this chapter, offering specific recommendations on how you can get a handle on them. We've mapped each recommendation to its specific corresponding NIST Framework subcategory so that you can dig deeper into the growing wealth of resources made available around the NIST Framework.

This chapter will present a general introduction to each of these categories, hitting the high points of what you need to know. We'll also give you recommended technical standards for each subcategory and suggest that you consult these standards for more details.

As you go through the chapter, bear in mind that there is no one-size-fits-all approach to security controls or developing security policies because each organization is unique. Each organization has its priorities, technical configurations, financial constraints, and operating philosophy. Some recommendations presented in this chapter may not apply to your organization, or may not apply now but might be of use in the future, or may need to be modified and tailored to fit your unique circumstances.

A. Identity Management, Authentication, and Access Control

Access control is the first and most crucial step in protecting your organization's networks and assets. It is simply the process through which your organization ensures that an authenticated user gains access to only what they are authorized to access and nothing else. In the words of the NIST

Framework, the outcome of access control is "access to assets and associated facilities is limited to authorized users, processes, or devices, and to authorized activities and transactions."

Before we proceed, it's helpful to make the distinction between authentication and authorization. Authentication is the act or process of determining that a user is who they say they are and gathering information on how they are accessing your systems. For example, Judy in accounting can access the payroll system on the company network using her login ID and password. However, when she tries to access the system from home, she has to provide a second form of authentication by typing in a passcode sent to her phone.

On the other hand, authorization is the act of determining the level of access an authorized user has to systems and data. Judy in accounting is authorized to access the payroll systems but she cannot update software in the network management systems. To effectively implement access control, your organization must first identify which systems need to have controlled access, and under what rules access should be granted.

Determining the systems for which you must control access is entirely contingent on what you deem most valuable or otherwise strategically important. Your risk assessment analysis can be useful in drawing up a list of systems for which access control should be applied and how. In terms of the rules that should apply to the various levels of access, some factors to consider are:

- Connection type
- CRUD enforcement (create, read-only, update, delete)
- Time of day
- Cascading authorization (some authorizations come with obligations for further actions)
- Global permissions
- Combination of privileges

Voices of Experience
On Granting Access

Watch Out for Layering Entitlements When Job Functions Change

By focusing on the identity and putting the user front and center, you think about the workflows to creating and managing the user's account. This is the entire user life cycle, often called the "hire to retire" process. Activating and disabling an account is easy. To make sure that there's segregation of duties, the more difficult part is when the user gets promoted or when the user moves from that accounts payable clerk role to being an accounts payable supervisor. You need to make sure that you are giving them the new rights while removing the old ones. Otherwise, you start layering entitlements on top of them. This can be a big problem, especially for a publicly traded company, especially if you get audits every year and you must comply with Sarbanes–Oxley (SOX).

Joe Klein, former CISO, Enersys & BillTrust

Ultimately, the goal of authorization is to employ the principle of "least privilege" necessary to perform job functions. This least privilege rule means that it's safer and more secure to give users only those privileges they need to complete the tasks covered by their role in the organization. For example, if a user account exists solely to perform back-ups, that account doesn't also gain the ability to implement software updates.

There are many appropriate steps to implement access control adequately. We'll go through a few of these in the following sections.

1. **Always Be Aware of Who Has Access to Which System, for Which Period of Time, and from Where the Access Is Granted** (PR.AC-1: Identities and credentials are issued, managed, verified, revoked, and audited for authorized devices, users, and processes.)

Organizations often have to manage many different system account types, from the individual, shared, group, guest, anonymous, developer, or service accounts. Generally speaking, you should restrict accounts by knowledge of passwords. Still, additional measures include restricting by time (temporary), restricting by geography (off-premises access), restricting by source (access control lists), and restricting by certificate (public/private key pairing so that only specific encrypted messages can be accessed).

In the language of the Cybersecurity Council, the objective of this aspect of access control is to "actively manage the life-cycle of system and application accounts, including their creation, use, dormancy, and deletion, and to minimize opportunities for attackers to leverage them."[1]

To establish access control, it's essential that your organization accurately tracks and builds into your account activation procedures all of the different system account characteristics mentioned above (and more) that may be specific to your unique circumstances. Ensure that you are consistent with the definition of authorization and users' access privileges defined for other security controls.

In addition to managing credentials for activating authorization, it's equally important that your organization establish procedures for ★deactivating★ authorizations, particularly where you set temporary accounts for short-term or emergency purposes. The activation of these temporary accounts often bypasses standard procedures and can get lost in the shuffle if you don't establish rigorous deactivation processes.

---

[1] CIS Security, Asset Monitoring and Control, https://www.cisecurity.org/controls/account-monitoring-and-control/#:~:text=CIS%20Control%2016This%20is%20a,for%20attackers%20to%20leverage%20them.

Relevant Technical Standards for PR.AC-1

Identities and credentials are issued, managed, verified, revoked, and audited for authorized devices, users, and processes

- CIS CSC 1, 5, 15, 16
- COBIT 5 DSS05.04, DSS06.03
- ISA 62443-2-1:2009 4.3.3.5.1
- ISA 62443-3-3:2013 SR 1.1, SR 1.2, SR 1.3, SR 1.4, SR 1.5, SR 1.7, SR 1.8, SR 1.9
- ISO/IEC 27001:2013 A.9.2.1, A.9.2.2, A.9.2.3, A.9.2.4, A.9.2.6, A.9.3.1, A.9.4.2, A.9.4.3
- NIST SP 800-53 Rev. 4 AC-1, AC-2, IA-1, IA-2, IA-3, IA-4, IA-5, IA-6, IA-7, IA-8, IA-9, IA-10, IA-11

---

2. Establish, Maintain, and Audit an Active Control List and Process for Who Can Physically Gain Access to Systems

(PR.AC-2: Physical access to assets is managed and protected.)

Establishing access control procedures is not a helpful activity unless your organization also establishes procedures that prevent unauthorized access, damage, or interference to your organization's systems. Therefore, it's crucial to develop a process of verifying who gains physical access to which systems. You can accomplish this process through a variety of means. For example, for gaining access to equipment, the user has to present a card key plus two-factor authentication such as a PIN or a fingerprint.

To maintain adequate physical access to systems, periodic audits of who gained access to which systems are helpful. You will also find it beneficial to keep an access control list containing all of the authorization credentials and the individuals to whom these credentials apply.

Relevant Technical Standards for PR.AC-2

Physical access to assets is managed and protected

- COBIT 5 DSS01.04, DSS05.05
- ISA 62443-2-1:2009 4.3.3.3.2, 4.3.3.3.8
- ISO/IEC 27001:2013 A.11.1.1, A.11.1.2, A.11.1.3, A.11.1.4, A.11.1.5, A.11.1.6, A.11.2.1, A.11.2.3, A.11.2.5, A.11.2.6, A.11.2.7, A.11.2.8
- NIST SP 800-53 Rev. 4 PE-2, PE-3, PE-4, PE-5, PE-6, PE-8

---

3. Establish Policies, Procedures, and Controls for Who Has Remote Access to Systems

(PR.AC-3: Remote access is managed.)

Managing remote access to systems is a crucial part of cybersecurity because the likelihood of unauthorized access increases when remote access to systems is involved. Remote access is simply the act of accessing organizational systems (by individuals or computer processes) through external networks such as the internet.

Your organization should establish formal remote access procedures, policies, and controls for all types of remote communications facilities, including virtual private networks and mobile devices, to determine who has access and what kind of access you give from remote locations.

An important distinction regarding remote access policies and procedures is warranted. In our earlier chapter on risk management, we discussed how you could establish remote access procedures for vendors and other third parties. However, in terms of access control, the remote access policies apply to organizational employees who use their personally owned devices or other privately owned devices in public facilities (such as hotel business centers) to access your systems.

Many organizations handle the problem of remote access by using virtual private networks (VPNs). New evolving solutions replace many VPN solutions using software-defined networking, which focuses on controlling access at the application layer rather than the network layer. A software-defined network can cut down on the complexity of designing and maintaining access control lists. Other methods to protect the organization from threats coming from remote access might include:

- mandatory "health" checks of an employee or other privately owned equipment,
- policy-based access control that assesses the device, the network that the user connects from, and the resources attempting to be accessed, and
- isolation techniques to limit remote access only to sections of the network based on business needs – traditional methods use jump-servers but, as mentioned, evolving solutions offer software-defined networking.

Relevant Technical Standards for PR.AC-3

Remote access is managed

- CIS CSC 12
- COBIT 5 APO13.01, DSS01.04, DSS05.03
- ISA 62443-2-1:2009 4.3.3.6.6
- ISA 62443-3-3:2013 SR 1.13, SR 2.6
- ISO/IEC 27001:2013 A.6.2.1, A.6.2.2, A.11.2.6, A.13.1.1, A.13.2.1
- NIST SP 800-53 Rev. 4 AC-1, AC-17, AC-19, AC-20, SC-15

---

4. **Make Sure That Users Have the Least Authority Possible to Perform Their Jobs and Ensure That at Least Two Individuals Are Responsible for a Task**

   (PR.AC-4: Access permissions are managed, incorporating the principles of least privilege and separation of duties.)

The least privilege principle states that users should access only the information and resources needed to do their jobs. The principle of separation of duties breaks down tasks so that no single person is in control.

An excellent example of the value of this separation of responsibilities might be the recent rise of spear phishing scams known as business e-mail compromise. These scams, in which the e-mail sender impersonates CEOs and CFOs who are putatively requesting wire transfers, have been targeting treasury and finance departments. The best practice in these situations is to designate the ability to request a wire transfer to one person. Still, approval for the actual funds' transfer is contingent on another person. This separation would require two people to fall prey to the scam.

Mismanagement of this access control aspect is an excellent way for attackers to access your systems and assets. In one prevalent attacker technique, a privileged user is a victim of a security attack such as malware delivered via phishing. If the user has access to sensitive information assets, the attacker also has access to these assets.

Another common technique is when an attacker uses a process of elimination or guessing to crack a user's password. The more accounts with access to sensitive assets, the greater the likelihood attackers will gain access to sensitive assets, allowing the miscreants to control the assets.

The following steps can be useful in alleviating these password access issues:

- Develop built-in operating systems that contain lists of accounts.
- Ban users with super privileges from surfing the web or reading e-mail on those accounts.
- Employ a privileged access management system that vaults passwords and offers check-in, check-out of account passwords. Users never know the password until you check them out. After they complete their work, you can change the passwords automatically.
- Enforce strong passwords and strong password protections.
- Implement additional authentication factors for privileged administrative accounts and any externally hosted or available applications on the internet (e.g., cloud, demilitarized zone applications, etc.).
- Limit access to privileged administrative accounts.
- Pro-tip: subscribe to HaveIBeenPwned.com and establish a process to regularly check to see if any e-mail accounts associated with domains you own show up on the list. Or check the built-in browser password checks that now appear in Chrome or Firefox. Enforce password resets for any accounts that you flag in any of these checks.

Relevant Technical Standards for PR.AC-4

Access permissions are managed, incorporating the principles of least privilege and separation of duties

- CIS CSC 3, 5, 12, 14, 15, 16, 18
- COBIT 5 DSS05.04
- ISA 62443-2-1:2009 4.3.3.7.3
- ISA 62443-3-3:2013 SR 2.1
- ISO/IEC 27001:2013 A.6.1.2, A.9.1.2, A.9.2.3, A.9.4.1, A.9.4.4, A.9.4.5
- NIST SP 800-53 Rev. 4 AC-1, AC-2, AC-3, AC-5, AC-6, AC-14, AC-16, AC-24

5. **Implement Network Security Controls on All Internal Communications, Denying Communications among Various Segments Where Necessary**
(PR.AC-5: Network integrity is protected (e.g., network segregation, network segmentation).)

Network integrity protection deals with network security management, which entails monitoring and implementing security controls on internal networks and communicating with external networks. For example, you can compartmentalize specific network resources, applications, and assets from other groups, and deny access across groups.

Although network segregation is a broad and complex topic outside this chapter's scope, it boils down to logically grouping network assets, resources, and applications together into compartmentalized areas or segments that don't trust one another. The benefits of segmenting or grouping assets, aside from improved access control, include:

- greater visibility into network traffic,
- protecting communications as they flow into and out of the organization, and
- setting default-deny policies on all intersegment communications.

For example, employees' private mobile communications that rely on organizational Wi-Fi connectivity can be segmented so that none of the organization's systems or data are affected or accessed. Without this segmentation, administrators would be unable to determine how much traffic over the organization's internet connections are due to employee mobile devices (which pose security risks), much less establish policies barring the private mobile devices from gaining a connection to core system functions.

Relevant Technical Standards for PR.AC-5

Network integrity is protected (e.g., network segregation, network segmentation)

- CIS CSC 9, 14, 15, 18
- COBIT 5 DSS01.05, DSS05.02
- ISA 62443-2-1:2009 4.3.3.4
- ISA 62443-3-3:2013 SR 3.1, SR 3.8
- ISO/IEC 27001:2013 A.13.1.1, A.13.1.3, A.13.2.1, A.14.1.2, A.14.1.3
- NIST SP 800-53 Rev. 4 AC-4, AC-10, SC-7

A WORD ABOUT FIREWALLS

Firewalls are a crucial sub-component of protecting network integrity, and, given the importance of firewalls, we'll spend a moment discussing them. In general, firewalls are technologies that segment parts of computer systems or networks to block unauthorized access but permit communications outward from the systems or networks. Instead of restricting unauthorized users, firewalls restrict unauthorized communications.

There are numerous types of firewalls and many different vendor products, so the details of how you implement firewalls will vary widely. Regardless of what technology you use or which vendor you select, there are some useful principles to consider when implementing firewalls within your organization:

- Create a policy consistent with your organization's risk management philosophy that specifies how firewalls should handle inbound and out-bound traffic.
- Identify all requirements that you should consider when determining which firewall to implement. Consider how your employees access resources and where the critical assets reside. Is a large population of your employees mobile? Is there heavy adoption of the cloud? It would help if you considered these types of questions because they can affect the solutions you need. If employees are rarely on site and the company uses cloud solutions, an on-premises firewall may not be a good fit.
- Create rule sets that implement the organization's firewall policy while supporting firewall performance. These rule sets will be dependent on the type of firewall you use and the specific firewall products you deploy.
- Manage firewall architectures, policies, software, and other components throughout the life of the firewall solution. The type of firewall you use can affect the security policies you enforce. If those policies change, you should review the firewall component of your protection strategy. It's also essential to examine firewall logs and log alerts to identify threats.

You can find more detailed information on installing, managing, and main-taining firewalls in the NIST special publication, *Guidelines on Firewalls and Firewall Policy*, Special Publication 800-41, Revision 1, http://nvlpubs.nist.gov/nistpubs/Legacy/SP/nistspecialpublication800-41r1.pdf.

6. Associate Activities with a Real Person or a Single Specific Entity
(PR.AC-6: Identities are proofed and bound to credentials and asserted in interactions.)

One of the biggest challenges in identity management is associating a set of online or other digital activities with a specific individual or entity. Although anonymity is helpful in many cases, there are situations where it is crucial to establish an association with a real-life subject reliably.

In these situations, good cybersecurity practice requires what is called iden-tity proofing. In this complex process, you take steps to ensure a user or an entity is who they claim to be to a certain level of certainty. This assurance includes either in-person or online presentation, validation, and verification of the minimum attributes necessary to accomplish identity proofing, such as pro-viding name, address, date of birth, e-mail address, phone number, passport, driver's license, photos, and even biometric data.

Once you proof an identity, you can bind other authenticated activities to that proof. For example, once a bank proves a customer's identity to open a checking account, that customer can launch an online payment application bound to the original identifying credentials supplied when opening the account.

Relevant Technical Standards for PR.AC-6

Identities are proofed and bound to credentials and asserted in interactions

- CIS CSC 16
- COBIT 5 DSS05.04, DSS05.05, DSS05.07, DSS06.03
- ISA 62443-2-1:2009 4.3.3.2.2, 4.3.3.5.2, 4.3.3.7.2, 4.3.3.7.4
- ISA 62443-3-3:2013 SR 1.1, SR 1.2, SR 1.4, SR 1.5, SR 1.9, SR 2.1
- ISO/IEC 27001:2013 A.7.1.1, A.9.2.1
- NIST SP 800-53 Rev. 4 AC-1, AC-2, AC-3, AC-16, AC-19, AC-24, IA-1, IA-2, IA-4, IA-5, IA-8, PE-2, PS-3

---

7. Use Single- or Multi-Factor Authentication Based on the Risk Involved in the Interaction

(PR.AC-7: Users, devices, and other assets are authenticated (e.g., single-factor, multi-factor) commensurate with the risk of the transaction (e.g., individuals' security and privacy risks and other organizational risks.)

As online and digital risks increase in number and grow more complicated, user authentication methods are growing more complex. It's impossible in the digital era to implement the authentication process with in-person or physical documentation to prove identity for users who want access to critical or sensitive resources.

Single-factor authentication, such as a user ID and password, has proven to be an insecure method for accessing important assets because it is vulnerable to malware attacks, replay attacks, offline brute force attacks, key logger Trojans, dictionary attacks, shoulder surfing, re-use of credentials stolen in massive data breaches, and many other threats.

On the other hand, multi-factor authentication represents multiple single-factor authentication methods and is generally considered more secure than single-factor authentication. Multi-factor authentication can combine user credentials (IDs and passwords) with mobile phone verification, e-mail verification, PINs, biometric markers such as fingerprints, physical security tokens, or keys such as USB sticks, and other methods.

It will help if you choose whether to deploy single-factor or multi-factor authentication for your systems and assets consistent with your organization's risk assessment analysis. You should consider giving greater preference to more robust authentication methods for those assets and systems most at risk and most likely to cause damage if malicious actors breach them.

Relevant Technical Standards for PR.AC-7

Users, devices, and other assets are authenticated (e.g., single-factor, multi-factor) commensurate with the risk of the transaction (e.g., individuals' security and privacy risks and other organizational risks)

- CIS CSC 1, 12, 15, 16
- COBIT 5 DSS05.04, DSS05.10, DSS06.10

- ISA 62443-2-1:2009 4.3.3.6.1, 4.3.3.6.2, 4.3.3.6.3, 4.3.3.6.4, 4.3.3.6.5, 4.3.3.6.6, 4.3.3.6.7, 4.3.3.6.8, 4.3.3.6.9
- ISA 62443-3-3:2013 SR 1.1, SR 1.2, SR 1.5, SR 1.7, SR 1.8, SR 1.9, SR 1.10
- ISO/IEC 27001:2013 A.9.2.1, A.9.2.4, A.9.3.1, A.9.4.2, A.9.4.3, A.18.1.4
- NIST SP 800-53 Rev. 4 AC-7, AC-8, AC-9, AC-11, AC-12, AC-14, IA-1, IA-2, IA-3, IA-4, IA-5, IA-8, IA-9, IA-10, IA-11

III. AWARENESS AND TRAINING

Securing and protecting systems and infrastructure requires a lot of skill and training. That's why one of the chief subcategories in the Protect function of the NIST Framework includes awareness and training guidelines and why one of the top goals of the National Initiative for Cybersecurity Education (NICE), a federal project that began in 2010, is initial and ongoing training for workers in cybersecurity.

As a side note, the increasing use of phishing assessments among all employees is an excellent method to educate and train the workforce about the dangers of phishing e-mails. In essence, your organization might consider sending test phishing e-mails to the workforce and then use the results of those e-mails to educate them on how to spot phishing e-mails.

Voices of Experience
On Awareness and Training

Training That Is Most Useful to Employees

One of the things we did at Ohio State is we really delved into how do you make advocates of people. One of the big things was this concept of pulling in social influences into your training. We worked with our mobile team to come up a platform which was new and exciting. Small bytes of information about security ideas that we called activities that people could choose to take. First of all we didn't make it mandatory. We encouraged people to go check the platform out and then we had topics within it.

Making Employees Embrace and Connect to Training

We have to make it something that would appeal to them personally, so the reality for us was people didn't care about cybersecurity. But they did care about their own data. They did care about their own banking. They cared about whether their kids were getting bullied online. They cared about privacy of their use of social media, those kinds of things.

Helen Patton, former Chief Information Security Officer, The Ohio State University

The NIST Framework provides subcategories under the awareness and training category, which all have the same outcome. What we'll touch on in this chapter is PR.AT-5, which concerns cybersecurity personnel's understanding of their roles and responsibilities, but in essence the same recommendations apply across all five of the NIST awareness and training subcategories.

A. Make Sure That Privileged Users and Security Personnel Understand Their Roles and Responsibilities

(PR.AT-5: Physical and cybersecurity personnel understand their roles and responsibilities.)

You must establish fundamental security skills among select asset users to improve your security posture. This skills development can entail installing or using formal or informal training programs and using standards for determining users' and personnel's qualifications.

Relevant Technical Standards for PR.AT-5

Physical and cybersecurity personnel understand their roles and responsibilities

- CIS CSC 17
- COBIT 5 APO07.03
- ISA 62443-2-1:2009 4.3.2.4.2
- ISO/IEC 27001:2013 A.6.1.1, A.7.2.2
- NIST SP 800-53 Rev. 4 AT-3, IR-2, PM-13

IV. DATA SECURITY

Nothing is more valuable to an organization's functioning than the data it maintains, which is why hackers seek out databases and other sources of data to steal from business, government, and non-profit organizations. Data security is simply the policies and procedures for protecting data when transmitted or "in transit" and when it's "at rest" or in storage. The NIST Framework defines data security as "information and records (data) are managed consistent with the organization's risk strategy to protect the confidentiality, integrity, and availability of information."

In short, any effective security program must protect the value and integrity of your organization's data. The data protection steps we'll touch on in this section of the chapter should go a long way to ensuring that your data – both in transit and at rest – is protected.

Before we begin, we should note that many organizations' data are accessible through database management systems (DBMS), which require managerial, technical, and physical controls consistent with the organization's risk assessment strategy.

A. Protect the Integrity of Active and Archived Databases

(PR.DS-1: Data-at-rest is protected.)

All organizations should institute mechanisms that address the security, integrity, and confidentiality of information in active and archived databases.

The integrity of data means that the data is complete without any alteration from its original state.

No single control can ultimately ensure your data integrity, but various techniques can help protect it. You can maintain the integrity of your databases by implementing several techniques, such as:

- Cryptography
- File-share scanning
- WORM (write once, read many discs that prevent erasure or alteration of data)
- Maintaining databases offsite and not online

Before implementing methods to protect your databases, it's helpful to identify and address potential sources of damage to data to select the best approach. In particular, users should familiarize themselves with the unique needs of protecting the vast amount of media stored in databases, often precious and copyrighted material, to ensure that the content cannot be accessed or altered.

Finally, if your organization chooses to use third-party off-site storage vendors, make sure to examine their security policies so that you can have the comfort of knowing that those policies are adequate for your needs.

Relevant Technical Standards for PR.DS-1

Data-at-rest is protected

- CIS CSC 13, 14
- COBIT 5 APO01.06, BAI02.01, BAI06.01, DSS04.07, DSS05.03, DSS06.06
- ISA 62443-3-3:2013 SR 3.4, SR 4.1
- ISO/IEC 27001:2013 A.8.2.3
- NIST SP 800-53 Rev. 4 MP-8, SC-12, SC-28

B. Protect the Confidentiality and Integrity of Corporate Data Once It Leaves Internal Networks

(PR.DS-2: Data-in-transit is protected.)

Communication between internal and external networks, also called data-in-transit, must be protected from unauthorized parties, including malicious hackers, through any one of several means, including encryption or using separate secure systems. Because communications are continually flowing into and out of a wide range of devices, including servers, mobile devices, tablets, printers, network-connected copiers, scanners, fax machines, and dozens of other devices, ensure your data protection plans encompass all of these forms of communications devices.

Besides the dozens of other specific devices that you should incorporate into data-in-transit security plans, you should think about data movement from an assortment of industry-specific devices and machines to more endpoints.

Many of these endpoints, particularly many vendor endpoints, do not offer acceptable encryption practices, such as HTTPS protection. It would help if you considered treating any data that flows through to endpoints that use bad encryption practices as confidential and take whatever steps necessary to protect the data.

Generally, when working with outside communications network providers that don't meet your security requirements, you should consider implementing compensating security controls to cover the deficiency.

Relevant Technical Standards for PR.DS-2

Data-in-transit is protected

- CIS CSC 13, 14
- COBIT 5 APO01.06, DSS05.02, DSS06.06
- ISA 62443-3-3:2013 SR 3.1, SR 3.8, SR 4.1, SR 4.2
- ISO/IEC 27001:2013 A.8.2.3, A.13.1.1, A.13.2.1, A.13.2.3, A.14.1.2, A.14.1.3
- NIST SP 800-53 Rev. 4 SC-8, SC-11, SC-12

C. Assure That Information Can Only Be Accessed by Those Authorized to Do So and Protect Hardware and Storage Media

(PR.DS-6: Integrity checking mechanisms are used to verify software, firmware, and information integrity.)

From the perspective of data and network security, we can define integrity as the assurance that information can only be accessed or modified by those authorized to do so. By maintaining strict authorization procedures, organizations can protect data integrity by making administrative functions of servers accessible only to network administrators.

Among the steps you can take in maintaining strict authorization procedures are:

- Restrict data access by implementing controls that make administrative functions on the server available only to administrators.
- Document all authorized users by level.
- Document admin procedures and maintenance activities.
- Consider file integrating monitoring solutions for critical information assets, particularly those stored in unsecured file shares, given the prevalence of network-propagating ransomware.

Moreover, physical protection is also key to data and network integrity. To keep assets physically protected, take steps to protect them from damage or interference. These steps can include keeping transmission media (such as cables and connectors) covered and protected to ensure that bad actors can't tap them and protecting hardware and storage media from power surges, electrostatic discharges, and magnetism.

Relevant Technical Standards for PR.DS-6

Integrity checking mechanisms are used to verify software, firmware, and information integrity

- CIS CSC 2, 3
- COBIT 5 APO01.06, BAI06.01, DSS06.02
- ISA 62443-3-3:2013 SR 3.1, SR 3.3, SR 3.4, SR 3.8
- ISO/IEC 27001:2013 A.12.2.1, A.12.5.1, A.14.1.2, A.14.1.3, A.14.2.4
- NIST SP 800-53 Rev. 4 SC-16, SI-7

D. Keep Your Development and Testing Environments Separate from Your Production Environment

(PR.DS-7: The development and testing environment(s) are separate from the production.)

Anyone who has ever developed a software system or even a website has learned this subcategory of the NIST Framework the hard way. Development and testing of new techniques, software, or web interfaces should always occur away from the production environment because development or testing systems might contain bugs that can wreck production systems' memory, CPUs, and content.

Suppose you introduce a faulty development or test system to the production environment. In that case, you risk damaging your organization's reputation and revenues, not to mention disrupting many personnel who have to deal with the problem. Depending on the damage caused by creating a development or test system in the production environment, you might have to spend substantial sums hiring contractors to do the clean-up.

Conducting development work or test work on production systems are two different activities. Development work allows developers to make changes and test out new options that they might not have been introduced into the production environment before. Developers often use integrated development environments that consist of various development tools such as Microsoft Visual Studio and other tools for logging or debugging.

Testing is identical to the production environment and could be a way for developers to test out updated software or enhance applications present in the production environment. Developers can install several different testing environments depending on the objectives pursued. Sometimes they want to test the performance of various parts of the production system. Sometimes they test the security hardiness of the production environment.

The bottom line is that to minimize the risk of business disruption, you should conduct both development and testing on systems separated from the production environment.

For further technical information on how best to separate development and test from the production environment, NIST has mapped this subcategory to the following standards:

Relevant Technical Standards for PR.DS-7

The development and testing environments(s) are separate from the production

- CIS CSC 18, 20
- COBIT 5 BAI03.08, BAI07.04
- ISO/IEC 27001:2013 A.12.1.4
- NIST SP 800-53 Rev. 4 CM-2

E.   Implement Checking Mechanisms to Verify Hardware Integrity
(PR.DS-8: Integrity checking mechanisms are used to verify hardware integrity.)

Ensuring the accuracy and integrity of hardware components in your systems is crucial to your organization's security. Therefore, it's helpful to implement checking mechanisms that periodically verify the integrity of the hardware.

Independent testing authorities can conduct this verification process, or you can run the checking mechanisms in-house. Either way, the following are just some considerations to bear in mind when conducting hardware verification tests:

- Test your hardware under conditions that simulate their expected real-life situations, including storage, operations, and maintenance environments.
- Ensure that the hardware conforms with local environmental requirements, including shelter, space, furnishings and fittings, electrical power supply, and relevant extremes of temperature, humidity, and pollution.
- Ensure that you have complete and appropriate documentation for the hardware.
- Verify that the hardware operates normally under abnormal conditions.

Relevant Technical Standards for PR.DS-8

Integrity checking mechanisms are used to verify hardware integrity

- COBIT 5 BAI03.05
- ISA 62443-2-1:2009 4.3.4.4.4
- ISO/IEC 27001:2013 A.11.2.4
- NIST SP 800-53 Rev. 4 SA-10, SI-7

V.   INFORMATION PROTECTION PROCESSES AND PROCEDURES

You should ideally develop all your information security programs according to processes, policies, and procedures. To be most effective, you should ensure that policies emanate from the organization's top level. In addition to policies that apply to top-level employees, including security personnel, you should establish specific guidelines for all workforce members, including staff, vendors, volunteers, and just about everybody in the organization. These policies should have procedures and expectations for workers to follow.

The NIST Framework puts it this way: "Security policies (that address purpose, scope, roles, responsibilities, management commitment, and coordination among organizational entities), processes, and procedures are maintained and used to manage protection of information systems and assets."

In this next section, we'll walk through some of the tasks needed to develop security program processes, procedures, and policies.

A. Create a Baseline of IT and OT Systems

(PR.IP-1 A baseline configuration of information technology/industrial control systems is created and maintained incorporating appropriate security principles (e.g., concept of least functionality).)

This subcategory's primary purpose is to foster an environment where organizations adopt baseline configurations of their IT and OT systems, keeping in mind some bedrock cybersecurity principles discussed later in the chapter, least privilege and least functionality. "Baseline configurations are documented, formally reviewed, and agreed-upon sets of specifications for information systems or configurations items within those systems."[2]

Baseline configurations serve as the basis for all future changes to the systems and are the most stable version. They can include "information about information system components (e.g., standard software packages installed on work computers, notebook computers, servers, network components, or mobile devices; current version numbers and patch information on operating systems and applications; and configuration settings/parameters), network topology, and the logical placement of those components within the system architecture."

In some contexts, baseline configurations serve to lay down the markers for permitted or prohibited processes. The bottom-line goal is to create a secure environment that the organization alters only after deliberation and consideration of the security principles that underpin that environment.

For more information on the topic of baseline configurations, NIST has mapped the following standards to this subcategory:

Relevant Technical Standards for PR.IP-1

A baseline configuration of information technology/industrial control systems is created and maintained incorporating security principles (e.g., concept of least functionality)

- CIS CSC 3, 9, 11
- COBIT 5 BAI10.01, BAI10.02, BAI10.03, BAI10.05

---

[2] NIST, NIST Special Publication 800-53 (Rev. 4) at https://nvd.nist.gov/800-53/Rev4/control/CM-2#:~:text=Baseline%20configurations%20are%20documented%2C%20formally,or%20changes%20to%20information%20systems.

- ISA 62443-2-1:2009 4.3.4.3.2, 4.3.4.3.3
- ISA 62443-3-3:2013 SR 7.6
- ISO/IEC 27001:2013 A.12.1.2, A.12.5.1, A.12.6.2, A.14.2.2, A.14.2.3, A.14.2.4
- NIST SP 800-53 Rev. 4 CM-2, CM-3, CM-4, CM-5, CM-6, CM-7, CM-9, SA-10

B. Manage System Configuration Changes in a Careful, Methodical Way

(PR.IP-3: Configuration change control processes are in place.)

This task is part of a much broader subject known as configuration management, a vast and complex discipline far more expansive than this chapter's scope. We'll spend some time boiling down critical aspects of configuration management that should be helpful to you, even if your organization doesn't have the resources to embrace many aspects of configuration management fully.

Configuration management is a technique for monitoring and controlling all forms of development activity. To monitor and control development activity, you should construct the system's basic structure through some sort of identification scheme. You should also put a management system into place to designate the organization's management level needed to make changes at various scheme layers.

Configuration management spells out the methods for controlling changes to assets throughout the assets' life cycles. Using a life-cycle process provides control over an organization's assets, which has several strategic security benefits, including:

- maintaining the integrity of system configurations so that you can make rational changes in an orderly way,
- keeping top management plugged in, and
- providing a basis for measurement.

You should assign each role in the configuration management process to one of three appropriate managers. First, a configuration manager should be designated who makes sure that each requirement of change management is carried out.

It's also helpful to designate a "baseline" manager to track changes in a change management ledger (CML) and maintain all products' libraries or records. The baseline manager ensures that all configuration items (CIs) in the product configuration management plan are accounted for and maintained according to a specified identification scheme.

Finally, a verification manager helps ensure that product integrity is maintained during the change process. The verification manager also maintains documentation of the change process and other vital tasks.

For any of these managers to perform their tasks, you should develop a configuration management scheme to establish the baseline. You should maintain the scheme throughout the life cycle of the asset. Each asset should have a product identification number in the scheme for easy reference and tracking.

Once you establish the baseline, good practice suggests that you make any changes to the baseline at the highest management level possible. For some organizations, this can be a complex and challenging task requiring management input at the top ranks. Once you build baseline configurations for critical assets, it's helpful to scan for changes to the baseline periodically.

And a final note: acceptable CI management practices call for:

- Only open ports/protocols necessary for devices to function.
- ALWAYS change default administrative account passwords.
- Deploy "switch user" functionality to access root accounts, such as sudo. This functionality means that higher priority users can gain control over lower priority users.

Relevant Technical Standards for PR.IP-3

Configuration change control processes are in place

- CIS CSC 3, 11
- COBIT 5 BAI01.06, BAI06.01
- ISA 62443-2-1:2009 4.3.4.3.2, 4.3.4.3.3
- ISA 62443-3-3:2013 SR 7.6
- ISO/IEC 27001:2013 A.12.1.2, A.12.5.1, A.12.6.2, A.14.2.2, A.14.2.3, A.14.2.4
- NIST SP 800-53 Rev. 4 CM-3, CM-4, SA-10

A WORD ABOUT PATCH MANAGEMENT

One crucial activity that falls under configuration management that we highlight is patch management or incorporating vendor software and firmware patches in a reasonable, risk-aware, and secure manner. Many recent high-profile security failures, most prominently that of credit rating agency Equifax, were due to failed patch management, which in turn was due to poor organizational configuration management practices and policies.

Although it might seem like vendor patches should be implemented immediately, patching system assets should proceed consistently and orderly as all system changes under your organization's configuration management policies. Consistent with your organization's risk management plan, you should develop a risk assessment process to evaluate vendor-released patches' criticality and applicability. This risk assessment should balance the potential downsides or risks of not patching the reported vulnerability against the extent of downtime and impaired functionality, and possible loss of data while you implement patches.

Keeping track of newly issued patches and conducting patch risk assessments can be an overwhelming task, particularly for an organization that uses a wide range of IT- and OT-specific technologies. Depending on your organization's size and complexity, it might be helpful to use an automated tool and maintain a database of monitored systems to evaluate which patches are critical, which ones are useful, and which ones are not needed. NIST has a guide to help steer you through the creation or adoption of automated patch management technologies: SP 800-40 Rev. 3, *Guide to Enterprise Patch Management Technologies* at https://csrc.nist.gov/publications/detail/sp/800-40/rev-3/final.

C. Perform Frequent Backups and Test Your Backup Systems Often

(PR.IP-4: Backups of information are conducted, maintained, and tested.)

Because the information in your databases is valuable and because all systems are prone to failure, maintaining up-to-date backups of databases and other important information is critical to resiliency in the event of a security attack, equipment failure, or human error. A backup is simply a copy of information from your systems to another device for recovery or archiving.

In the event of a failure or attack, important information can be copied from the backup media into your production system in a process called data restoration. The following suggestions ensure that your backup plan will be available in those cases where you need to perform a data restoration:

- Implement a system for periodically checking to ensure that backups are taking place properly.
- Ensure the backup system receives the same protection level as the original data based on its value.
- Keep ongoing accurate records of how you perform backups.
- Keep backups in off-site storage away from the original systems, so they are not subject to the same damage of failure or attacks. (Make sure the facility meets your security standards!) This distance is significant in incidents that involve ransomware attacks.

Relevant Technical Standards for PR.IP-4

Backups of information are conducted, maintained, and tested

- CIS CSC 10
- COBIT 5 APO13.01, DSS01.01, DSS04.07
- ISA 62443-2-1:2009 4.3.4.3.9
- ISA 62443-3-3:2013 SR 7.3, SR 7.4
- ISO/IEC 27001:2013 A.12.3.1, A.17.1.2, A.17.1.3, A.18.1.3
- NIST SP 800-53 Rev. 4 CP-4, CP-6, CP-9

D. Create a Plan That Focuses on Ensuring That Assets and Personnel Will Be Able to Continue to Function in the Event of a Crippling Attack or Disaster

(PR.IP-9: Response plans (Incident Response and Business Continuity) and recovery plans (Incident Recovery and Disaster Recovery) are in place and managed.)

Response plans and disaster recovery plans are at the core of cybersecurity preparedness. Response plans, more often referred to as business continuity plans, are the crux of preserving organizational resiliency during extreme crises.

The flip side of response plans or business continuity plans is disaster recovery, and the two are often referred to as one concept – business continuity/disaster recovery. Disaster recovery is simply the process after which an organization resumes functioning after a disaster.

You should develop business continuity/disaster recovery plans to ensure that personnel and assets are available, protected, and able to function during and after extreme situations. The details of these plans are dependent on the organization's activities, but some factors to consider are:

1. How employees will communicate.
2. Where employees will go.
3. How to keep core functions operational in the event of a severe attack.

Relevant Technical Standards for PR.IP-9

Response plans (Incident Response and Business Continuity) and recovery plans (Incident Recovery and Disaster Recovery) are in place and managed

- CIS CSC 19
- COBIT 5 APO12.06, DSS04.03
- ISA 62443-2-1:2009 4.3.2.5.3, 4.3.4.5.1
- ISO/IEC 27001:2013 A.16.1.1, A.17.1.1, A.17.1.2, A.17.1.3
- NIST SP 800-53 Rev. 4 CP-2, CP-7, CP-12, CP-13, IR-7, IR-8, IR-9, PE-17

VI. MAINTENANCE

The development and documentation of system maintenance procedures and policies are critical to protecting your organization's ongoing operations. There are no blueprints for these policies and procedures, which can vary widely. But it is essential to develop a formal, documented information system maintenance policy that aligns with the policies your organization has established. At the same time, it's necessary to keep the maintenance policy updated with any changes in your system's IT or security maintenance programs.

Maintenance of assets encompasses all types of care for all kinds of components, not just IT assets, including:

- system software and business applications,
- network devices including scanners, copiers, printers, and voice-activated machines, and
- OT-specific software and devices.

For all of these organizational assets (and more), it's critical to establish who is responsible for maintenance, maintenance tools, and remote assets.

In this section of the chapter, we'll talk about how to perform maintenance tasks and repairs promptly and how to manage maintenance and diagnostic activities for third parties upon which your organization relies.

A. Perform Maintenance and Repair of Assets and Log Activities Promptly

(PR.MA-1: Maintenance and repair of organizational assets is performed and logged in a timely manner, with approved and controlled tools.)

The primary way to perform maintenance and repair of assets promptly is to ensure your organization schedules, performs, documents, and reviews records of maintenance and repairs on all system components based on what manufacturers or vendors define in their specifications, as well as your organizational requirements.

To achieve optimal maintenance, you should consider the following factors:

- Ensure your organization is in charge of all maintenance procedures, whether they are performed on site or remotely.
- Designate an employee who explicitly authorizes the removal of systems or system assets for off-site maintenance and repairs.
- Inspect and sanitize all media that are removed off site for repairs.
- When making repairs, check for all potentially impacted security controls to ensure they are still fully operational after performing maintenance and repairs.
- Establish a process for authorizing maintenance and repair personnel.
- Maintain a list of third-party personnel and maintenance organizations.

Relevant Technical Standards for PR.MA-1

Maintenance and repair of organizational assets is performed and logged in a timely manner, with approved and controlled tools

- COBIT 5 BAI03.10, BAI09.02, BAI09.03, DSS01.05
- ISA 62443-2-1:2009 4.3.3.3.7
- ISO/IEC 27001:2013 A.11.1.2, A.11.2.4, A.11.2.5, A.11.2.6
- NIST SP 800-53 Rev. 4 MA-2, MA-3, MA-5, MA-6

B. Develop Criteria for Authorizing, Monitoring, and Controlling All Maintenance and Diagnostic Activities for Third Parties

(PR.MA-2: Remote maintenance of organizational assets is approved, logged, and performed in a manner that prevents unauthorized access.)

It is widespread for many organizations to outsource maintenance and repair to third-party vendors. If your organization uses third parties for maintenance and repair procedures, ensure that the maintenance policy spells out criteria for authorizing, monitoring, and controlling all maintenance activities. These activities should be consistent with your organization's policies.

Voices of Experience
On Removable Media

Overlook Removable Media at Your Own Peril

Removable media are often overlooked as a risk. When you look at awareness and training around phishing attempts by adversaries, you will hear countless stories about the conference attendee that goes to a booth and picks up a flash drive in a fishbowl or they will find a flash drive on the ground walking into their office. They simply plug it into their computer. There are so many times that a ransomware or a type of commodity malware was executed just by plugging in that flash drive. It is basic, but locking that down is still a highly effective control.

Joe Klein, former CISO, Enersys & BillTrust

Relevant Technical Standards for PR.MA-2

Remote maintenance of organizational assets is approved, logged, and performed in a manner that prevents unauthorized access

- CIS CSC 3, 5
- COBIT 5 DSS05.04
- ISA 62443-2-1:2009 4.3.3.6.5, 4.3.3.6.6, 4.3.3.6.7, 4.3.3.6.8
- ISO/IEC 27001:2013 A.11.2.4, A.15.1.1, A.15.2.1
- NIST SP 800-53 Rev. 4 MA-4

VII.   PROTECTIVE TECHNOLOGY

This element of protecting your organization's assets deals with defining controls for protection settings that technical mechanisms can implement, often referred to as technical security architecture. In the parlance of the NIST Cybersecurity Framework, "Technical security solutions are managed to ensure the security and resilience of systems and assets, consistent with related policies, procedures, and agreements."

A.   Restrict the Use of Certain Types of Media On Your Systems
(PR.PT-2: Removable media is protected and its use restricted according to policy.)

Computerized media (as opposed to non-computerized media such as paper) are often used to knowingly or innocently inject malware into virtually every kind of system. It is helpful to restrict the use of specific devices on your plans.
    Among the devices for which you might want to draw up restrictions are:

- diskettes
- magnetic tapes
- external or removable hard drives

- flash drives
- compact discs
- smartphones
- tablets
- laptops
- organization-specific mobile or removable gear

Relevant Technical Standards for PR.PT-2

Removable media is protected and its use restricted according to policy

- CIS CSC 8, 13
- COBIT 5 APO13.01, DSS05.02, DSS05.06
- ISA 62443-3-3:2013 SR 2.3
- ISO/IEC 27001:2013 A.8.2.1, A.8.2.2, A.8.2.3, A.8.3.1, A.8.3.3, A.11.2.9
- NIST SP 800-53 Rev. 4 MP-2, MP-3, MP-4, MP-5, MP-7, MP-8

B. Wherever Possible, Limit Functionality to a Single Function Per Device (Least Functionality)

(PR.PT-3: The principle of least functionality is incorporated by configuring systems to provide only essential capabilities.)

Voices of Experience
On Least Functionality

Turn on Only Those Services Needed

The principle of least functionality relates to the computers themselves. Here you should only be turning on the services, opening ports, and installing the software that is needed. One organization where I was a cybersecurity executive when I first came in, I asked about the images that they used and was told they were provided by Microsoft with the default installation of Windows 7. My response was "no". When you install Windows, the default functionality is excessive. Look toward the available hardening guides to start with a basic build then turn components on afterwards. Turning on a service is quite easy. Having a live server that is used in production and hardening it after the fact is extremely painful.

Joe Klein, former CISO, Enersys & BillTrust

Many system components can serve multiple functions, but the principle of least functionality, whereby a device serves a single process (for example, a server can be an e-mail server or a web server but not both combined), can help you better manage authorized privileges to the services the device supports. Moreover, offering multiple services over a single device increases risk.

If you do offer multiple services over a single device, it is helpful to conduct periodic reviews to determine which services you can eliminate from the device. Finally, removing unnecessary ports or protocols can help maximize the least functionality status of your devices.

Relevant Technical Standards for PR.PT-3

The principle of least functionality is incorporated by configuring systems to provide only essential capabilities

- CIS CSC 3, 11, 14
- COBIT 5 DSS05.02, DSS05.05, DSS06.06
- ISA 62443-2-1:2009 4.3.3.5.1, 4.3.3.5.2, 4.3.3.5.3, 4.3.3.5.4, 4.3.3.5.5, 4.3.3.5.6, 4.3.3.5.7, 4.3.3.5.8, 4.3.3.6.1, 4.3.3.6.2, 4.3.3.6.3, 4.3.3.6.4, 4.3.3.6.5, 4.3.3.6.6, 4.3.3.6.7, 4.3.3.6.8, 4.3.3.6.9, 4.3.3.7.1, 4.3.3.7.2, 4.3.3.7.3, 4.3.3.7.4
- ISA 62443-3-3:2013 SR 1.1, SR 1.2, SR 1.3, SR 1.4, SR 1.5, SR 1.6, SR 1.7, SR 1.8, SR 1.9, SR 1.10, SR 1.11, SR 1.12, SR 1.13, SR 2.1, SR 2.2, SR 2.3, SR 2.4, SR 2.5, SR 2.6, SR 2.7
- ISO/IEC 27001:2013 A.9.1.2
- NIST SP 800-53 Rev. 4 AC-3, CM-7

C.   Implement Mechanisms to Achieve Resilience on Shared Infrastructure

(PR.PT-5: Mechanisms (e.g., failsafe, load balancing, hot swap) are implemented to achieve resilience requirements in normal and adverse situations.)

Resilience is critical to coping with incidents that could impede your operations, from minor incidents to catastrophic events. Achieving resilience is a significant effort that results from extensive planning for a host of activities, including prevention, protection, response, and recovery efforts.

Because modern technology networks typically serve as shared infrastructure initially designed for a limited set of services but are increasingly adapted to run multiple services not envisioned originally, you should develop and implement mechanisms so that failure of individual services don't cascade to cause failures among other services.

Among the mechanisms that you can implement to help achieve resilience requirements in every day and adverse situations are:

- **Fail-safe**: Fail-safe is an engineering concept holding that in situations with composite components, such as shared infrastructure, you should design the composite so that the parts fail in a "safe" way not to bring down the entire infrastructure.
- **Load Balancing**: Load balancing is a technique that distributes workloads across multiple computing resources such as computers, disk drives, CPUs, and other assets to optimize resource use, minimize response time, increase availability of applications, and prevent overloading any computing resource. Load balancing has traditionally been accomplished with hardware appliances but increasingly is achieved with software-defined technology.
- **Hot-Swap**: A hot swap is replacing a system component, whether a computer, a hard drive or even a power supply, while the system using it continues its operations.

> ## Relevant Technical Standards for PR.PT-5
>
> **Mechanisms (e.g., failsafe, load balancing, hot swap) are implemented to achieve resilience requirements in normal and adverse situations**
>
> - COBIT 5 BAI04.01, BAI04.02, BAI04.03, BAI04.04, BAI04.05, DSS01.05
> - ISA 62443-2-1:2009 4.3.2.5.2
> - ISA 62443-3-3:2013 SR 7.1, SR 7.2
> - ISO/IEC 27001:2013 A.17.1.2, A.17.2.1
> - NIST SP 800-53 Rev. 4 CP-7, CP-8, CP-11, CP-13, PL-8, SA-14, SC-6

SUMMARY

Here are some of the central lessons about user and network infrastructure planning and management that we've learned from this chapter:

- Access control, which ensures that a user is who they say they are (authenticated) and has access to only what they should access (authorized), is the first step in protecting an organization's systems and assets.
- Restrict user account access by several crucial factors, including time (permanent or temporary), geography (in-house versus external), type of content (confidential versus non-confidential), and other factors that shape your organization.
- Develop a process of who should gain physical access to systems.
- Establish formal remote access procedures, policies, and controls for all types of remote communications facilities.
- Follow the principle of least privilege and separation of duties, with users having access to only those resources they need to do their jobs and break down tasks so that a single person is in control.
- Protect your organization through network segmentation, grouping network resources, applications, and assets into specific groups.
- Use identity proofing to be certain that individuals are who they say they are and then bind authenticated activities to that proof.
- Consider multi-factor authentication for assets and systems most at risk.
- Ensure that users understand their roles and responsibilities through awareness training.
- Choose from several different methods to protect data-at-rest and data-in-transit.
- Use integrity checking mechanisms so that information can only be accessed or modified by those authorized to do so.
- Make sure your development and testing mechanisms are kept separate from your production environment.
- Implement checking mechanisms that periodically verify the integrity of your hardware.
- Create a baseline of systems that reverts to known secure versions and manage configuration changes in a careful, systematic way.
- Perform frequent back-ups, test your backup systems often and keep your backup systems off site.

- Create plans for personnel to function in the event of an attack.
- Perform maintenance of assets and log activities.
- Develop criteria for authorizing, monitoring, and controlling all maintenance activities of third parties.
- Restrict certain types of media use (e.g., thumb drive) on your network.
- Limit functionality to a single use per device.
- Develop and implement mechanisms so that failure of individual services don't cascade to cause failures among other services.

CHAPTER QUIZ

Now we're going to give you a short quiz that tests what you learned in the chapter using the scenario we presented initially. You can find the answers at the end of the book.

1. **Which of the following made Major Motors' recovery from the attack take longer than it should have? (Select One)**
   a. The company's databases were not adequately protected.
   b. The company didn't use firewalls, or the hackers wouldn't have gained access to assets.
   c. The company didn't maintain at least some of its critical backup databases off site.

2. **Which two essential steps in managing authorization credentials did the company miss?**
   a. The company failed to establish formal remote access procedures.
   b. The company failed to maintain an up-to-date access control list that contains all of the authorization credentials and the individuals to whom these credentials apply.
   c. The company failed to deauthorize Alan's temporary super-user account when it was no longer needed.

3. **Which of the following protective principles could have averted the company's disaster altogether?**
   a. The principle of least functionality.
   b. The principle of least privilege.

4. **Which of the following access control policies *might* have averted hackers from attaining access to Alan's credentials? (Select One)**
   a. The company should have required Alan to use a VPN even while he was playing his video game.
   b. The company should have conducted a "health check" on Alan's computer if he had permission to work remotely using it.
   c. The company should have segmented the network so that Alan couldn't access anything from his home computer.

ESSENTIAL READING ON NETWORK MANAGEMENT

Ciprian Rusen, User Accounts, Groups, Permissions and Their Role in Sharing, *How-to-Geek*, Updated April 30, 2019, at https://www.howtogeek.com/school/windows-network-sharing/lesson1.

Nicolas Mayer and Jocelyn Aubert, A Risk Management Framework for Security and Integrity of Networks and Services, *Journal of Risk Research*, June 24, 2020, at https://www.tandfonline.com/doi/full/10.1080/13669877.2020.1779786.

Jessica Dawson and Robert Tomson, The Future Cybersecurity Workforce: Going Beyond Technical Skills for Successful Cyber Performance, *Frontiers in Psychology*, June 12, 2018, at https://www.ncbi.nlm.nih.gov/pmc/articles/PMC6005833.

CHAPTER 3

Tools and Techniques for Detecting Cyber Incidents

Overview of Chapter and Objective

This chapter aims to help the reader describe effective techniques for detecting cyber incidents or attacks, establish best approaches for monitoring systems to detect incidents, and plan for the development of organizational processes for detecting incidents.

Olivia settled into her office early that day at 8:00 a.m., hoping to catch up on the news before starting the daily system maintenance tasks she undertook as a junior systems administrator at her non-profit, non-governmental organization (NGO). She checked out Google News, the New York Times, and then moved on to the Mapleton Daily Gazette's home page, which she considered the best local news source. The paper's reporters were particularly excellent in covering the city's local government.

She clicked on the Gazette's bookmark below her browser bar, and nothing appeared on the screen. Must have made a mistake, she thought, so she clicked on it again. Nothing. Then she manually typed the URL into the browser bar. Still nothing. She tried again. This time the paper's home page appeared. Metropolitan Broadband, the NGO's broadband provider, must be working on the network again and causing intermittent outages, Olivia thought. She scanned the newspaper's home page, and nothing interested her, so she turned to her e-mail.

She bolted upright when she saw thirty alerts from her anomaly detection system, with more pouring in every second. The alerts warned of two things: a spike in "503 service unavailable" instances for the organization's website and a

Cybersecurity Risk Management: Mastering the Fundamentals Using the NIST Cybersecurity Framework, First Edition. Cynthia Brumfield and Brian Haugli.
© 2022 Cynthia Brumfield and Brian Haugli. Published 2022 by John Wiley & Sons, Inc.

surge of requests from DNS addresses outside the usual geographic locations her organization attracted.

She opened the dashboard for the anomaly detection system. She saw that her organization's website had experienced five thousand instances of "503 service unavailable" messages in the past 30 minutes, which far exceeded the usual five cases per month. Moreover, the DNS addresses outside the top 10 geographic locations that usually visit the organization's website were two thousand times the amount they should be.

Olivia immediately recognized that these anomalies meant someone had leveled a distributed denial-of-service (DDoS) attack at her organization, and the attack was likely a big one – a domain name system (DNS) amplification attack. She knew that an attack like this could take the organization's website down for days, which could eat into revenues and donations, not to mention generate lousy press and anger against the parent organization's leaders. Olivia and the rest of the NGO's staff had suspected that some discontented group or person could aim a significant DDoS attack at the NGO because of its frequent controversial stances. That's why they were ready for such an eventuality.

She alerted the team to handle significant attacks like this, including the NGO's technology vice president, the general manager, the general counsel, and her subordinate, the organization's webmaster. But Olivia knew just what to do.

Months earlier, the NGO had switched to a new cloud content delivery network and cloud services provider who had walked her through their security capabilities and demonstrated a unique solution for heading off DDoS attacks at the outset. She called her contact at the company, who launched a new "red alert" system for allocating resources to ward off major DDoS attacks.

Within minutes, the organization's website was operating normally, and the onslaught of alerts in Olivia's inbox diminished. Over the next couple of weeks, the NGO team responsible for handling how attacks are detected and mitigated conducted a review and issued a report to all relevant personnel. This review offered an assessment of how the organization mitigated the incident and detailed steps for managing a similar incident in the future. Olivia, in particular, received praise for how prepared she was for the incident and how well she handled it.

INTRODUCTION

Welcome to Tools and Techniques for Detecting a Cyber Incidents. This chapter will help you gain skills that allowed Olivia to navigate a significant incident successfully.

We will introduce you to some key concepts for detecting cyber incidents, including:

- the importance of anomalies in the functioning of your systems and devices and how to detect them,
- how to establish monitoring systems that spot anomalies and events on an automated basis, and
- how to develop sound approaches to establishing organizational processes around detecting anomalies and events.

No technology system is secure if the organization does not have the means for first detecting a cyberattack. Before we learn how to catch a cyberattack, we'll spend a few minutes on a bit of background.

WHAT IS AN INCIDENT?

The very notion of a cyberattack justifiably strikes fear in the heart of most technologists. Internet protocol technology appears in not only traditional IT and communications technology; it also appears throughout OT-specific systems, as well as home appliances, automobiles, stoplights, security cameras, and even clothing. Therefore, the attack surface for cyber intrusions and destruction grows exponentially every day.

> **Voices of Experience**
> *On Why Detect Is "Right of Boom"*
>
> **Detect Looks for Weakness Exploitations**
>
> *When I look at the NIST cybersecurity framework, I see these different words like identify, protect, detect, respond, recover. The way that I look at the distinction is by creating this noticeably clear division between left and right of boom [before and after an incident]. So, on the functions about identify and protect, that is left of boom. Boom occurs between protect and detect. Detect, respond, recover is right of boom. When it comes to vulnerabilities, they are a structural weakness. Structural weaknesses are things that you find left of boom. Exploitation against those vulnerabilities is something that happens right of boom and when something gets exploited you want to go discover the exploitation.*
>
> *Here lies the ability for us to really distinguish the meaning of identify versus detect. When it comes to the function of identify, which is left of boom, we are trying to discover these exposed weaknesses that we have in our environment. When it comes to right of boom, and the function of detect, we are looking for exploitation against those weaknesses.*
>
> Sounil Yu, Author of the Cyber Defense Matrix, former Chief Security Scientist of Bank of America

The term cyberattack is a moving target as digital threats multiply. For this chapter's purpose, we define "cyberattack" as an attempt to bypass security mechanisms put in place for IT and OT systems, to otherwise use an IT or OT system without authorization, or to abuse existing privileges. Most cybersecurity professionals draw sharp lines around what constitutes attacks, preferring such cybersecurity incidents as unauthorized access to be called just that, "incidents," rather than the more inflammatory term "attacks."

To detect exploitation of assets or "cyberattacks," it's vital to have ethical rules and security controls in place. This chapter will walk you through some of the most critical elements of these rules and controls.

I. DETECT

Detecting a cyber incident has become an ever-increasing challenge, particularly for large organizations, because of continuous change in the various systems used within the organization. Threat actors can hide their tracks within what appear to be ever-more-complex processes, with indicators of an attack or intrusion shifting constantly. Detecting anomalous or destructive system changes amid thousands, tens of thousands, or even millions of routine changes is the key to identifying a malicious cyber incident and potentially saving your organization from complete operational failure.

Cybercriminals can hide their tracks through disguise, obfuscation, and increasingly innovative methods that take advantage of undiscovered vulnerabilities, also known as "zero days." Therefore, the most critical function of the NIST Framework in detecting a malicious cyber incident is, aptly enough, the Detect function.

We'll walk you through crucial categories and subcategories of the Detect function so that you can understand:

- what anomalies and events are and how to detect them,
- how to establish monitoring systems to spot anomalies and events on an automated basis, and
- how to develop sound approaches to establishing organizational processes around detecting anomalies and events.

Before we move on to more details about anomalies and events, it's important to highlight that one noteworthy trend in cybersecurity defense is the rise of community and commercial threat intelligence feeds. These feeds enable dynamic searching for malicious changes (also called indicators of compromise) such as IP addresses associated with malicious attacks, malware file names and hashes, and specific attack vectors. Many organizations have figured out how to ingest these feeds to enhance their automated intrusion detection systems.

These systems can help you gain real-time knowledge across assets, including understanding when malicious changes occur. Threat intelligence feeds can help organizations respond to cyberattacks more quickly and shift resources where needed in response to attack patterns. We'll return to the topic of threat intelligence and intrusion detection systems later.

A. Anomalies and Events

To detect a cyber incident, you should first implement controls that detect anomalies and grasp the events' potential impact. The outcome of this component in the NIST Framework is defined as "anomalous activity is detected in a timely manner and the potential impact of events is understood." By their very definition, anomalies are low-probability events, outliers, surprises, and exceptions that happen so infrequently that most IT experts can't prepare for them, making them very hard to detect.

An excellent example of anomaly detection is how banks catch fraudulent users. Over the years, banks have developed anomaly detection systems that sniff out fraud in credit and debit card use and establish norms that indicate unusual patterns or locations of purchases, often on a customer-by-customer basis. When violated, the banks' fraud departments are alerted and can freeze accounts and notify customers. Anything that appears to be suspicious, whether it is a pattern of purchases, locations of purchases, or even types of purchases, is fed into banking anomaly detection systems for further analysis and action.

To detect anomalies, however, a baseline of what is normal has to be established first. Using the banking example, a bank might determine that a $1 charge by any customer in three different cities within a five-minute frame is not a regular expenditure and will flag those charges as anomalies. Some customers, however, might have legitimate reasons for incurring single dollar charges across multiple cities within a short time frame. In those cases, banks' anomaly detection systems can ignore those transactions for those customers.

For anomaly detection systems to be effective and avoid sending too many alerts, a method for detecting anomalies must be based on a classification system that determines the difference between a "good" anomaly and a "bad" anomaly. You should continually modify any anomaly detection system you use to distinguish between the two. For example, the system might flag a new computer added to a network at first as an anomaly with alerts sent to IT staff. But, when the system is updated to accept the new computer as standard, it sends no alert.

This section of the chapter will walk you through some of the basic concepts of detecting and managing anomalous events.

1. **Establish Baseline Data for Normal, Regular Traffic Activity and Standard Configuration for Network Devices**
   (DE.AE-1: A baseline of network operations and expected data flow for users and systems is established and managed.)

Before any anomaly can be detected, it is fundamental to determine what is "normal" by establishing baseline data so that you can track deviations from that data.

Voices of Experience
On Anomalies and Events

Start Off with a Strong Foundation

For anomalies and events, we want to be looking at what's happening in our environment. It's interesting to look at the wording that NIST uses, "ensure a baseline." You want to start off with a strong foundation. My role in a security engineering organization is to look at every source and really think about what we expect to see there. You build out your expectations from different sources. We should have started with asset management to have a sense of everything that we're supposed to be watching in our environment. I know that a significant portion of our systems are not even talking to us at all. Maybe the agents were never installed, or the agents were installed, and they had an issue or the operating system shut them down, or there was a network problem between the system and wherever it is that you're storing these events and the logs aren't coming in. The worst time to find out this is happening is when you have an incident.

Omer Singer, Head of Cyber Security Strategy, Snowflake

Establishing baseline data requires tracking many different attributes across multiple dimensions, including normal host behavior, normal user behavior, application behavior, and numerous other factors, including external factors such as IP reputation. Time is also a factor in establishing the baseline. For example, suppose a user legitimately accesses a file over and over again over weeks. In that case, that might be an anomaly not captured if the baseline time-frame is only a week for tracking incidents of that file access.

Although we're using the term anomaly, a more accurate explanation might be "pattern of contrast" rather than static data points of "normal" and "abnor-mal." Attackers can quickly adapt to static baselines, but dynamic patterns that are tracked over time and continually updated can help thwart attacker efforts to elude detection.

A frequently cited example of this pattern of contrasts is the use of dynamic DNS (domain name system) services. When the use of these services is at a low of 0.5% of regular DNS traffic, an increase to 5% is an anomaly that you should investigate because bad actors have repeatedly used dynamic DNS as part of malware campaigns.

Another good example is monitoring outbound server connections that follow a set interval. For instance, if you discover a service or server calls out precisely every 10 minutes to a set of IPs, this might be an indicator of a com-promised system contacting its command and control (C&C) master.

Anomalies or patterns of contrast can apply to anything across your techni-cal assets and are highly contingent on your organization's systems, configura-tion, personnel, hardware and software assets, and many other factors. Some examples might include:

- a database server that suddenly has a lot of outbound traffic,
- a workstation trying to connect to many other hosts at once,
- a file server busy in the middle of the night when it usually is idle,
- firewall hits from a country with which your organization does no business, and
- one of your assets suddenly points to a new IP address that it had not pointed to before.

Relevant Technical Standards for DE.AE-1

A baseline of network operations and expected data flows for users and systems is established and managed

- CIS CSC 1, 4, 6, 12, 13, 15, 16
- COBIT 5 DSS03.01
- ISA 62443-2-1:2009 4.4.3.3
- ISO/IEC 27001:2013 A.12.1.1, A.12.1.2, A.13.1.1, A.13.1.2
- NIST SP 800-53 Rev. 4 AC-4, CA-3, CM-2, SI-4

---

2. **Monitor Systems with Intrusion Detection Systems and Establish a Way of Sending and Receiving Notifications of**

Detected Events; Establish a Means of Verifying, Assessing, and Tracking the Source of Anomalies

(DE.AE-2: Detected events are analyzed to understand attack targets and methods.)

You should perform two tasks when detecting anomalies:

- Monitor systems with tools known as intrusion detection systems.
- Send and receive notifications of detected anomalies.

These tasks are challenging because many (if not most) administrators don't know the type of network traffic allowed in their systems. Other potential problems include:

- External parties, such as vendors, may block intrusion detection traffic.
- Networks must continue to operate while intrusion detection systems run.
- Intrusion detection systems often spit out misleading, uninformative, or false-positive messages.

Therefore, the organization's customization is required for the intrusion detection system to help these and many other challenges.

Once an anomaly is detected, technical personnel should:

- verify, assess, and track the source of the anomaly and
- assess the incident's magnitude and consequences.

Endpoint detection and response (EDR) platforms have emerged in the past decade to bring these capabilities into the hands of more organizations. The idea is that a resident software agent monitors processes, connections, and behavior on each host. These are each logged and stored before being presented on dashboards and other analytical tools to administrators. When any abnormal activity is detected, the agent allows the administrator to address the issue almost surgically. Administrators also can find similar detections across other systems with agents installed, shut off network connectivity altogether on impacted systems, or continue to monitor malicious behavior to determine the attackers' actual targets.

Based on the risk assessment that the organization has conducted, you might deem some incidents as unimportant because the cost of addressing the incident outweighs its potential risk. For others, simple solutions might be available, such as turning off ports or reinstalling the software.

Once the anomaly is detected, verified, and its impact assessed, it helps identify the anomaly source. Often your organizational knowledge is enough to identify the source of a malicious incident. Sometimes, technical personnel have to collaborate with specialists, such as forensics experts, to determine the problem's source. Other times technical personnel may choose to simulate the incident in a contained and safe way to determine its origin.

Relevant Technical Standards for DE.AE-2

Detected events are analyzed to understand attack targets and methods

- CIS CSC 3, 6, 13, 15
- COBIT 5 DSS05.07
- ISA 62443-2-1:2009 4.3.4.5.6, 4.3.4.5.7, 4.3.4.5.8
- ISA 62443-3-3:2013 SR 2.8, SR 2.9, SR 2.10, SR 2.11, SR 2.12, SR 3.9, SR 6.1, SR 6.2
- ISO/IEC 27001:2013 A.12.4.1, A.16.1.1, A.16.1.4
- NIST SP 800-53 Rev. 4 AU-6, CA-7, IR-4, SI-4

A WORD ABOUT ANTIVIRUS SOFTWARE

Antivirus software is a monitoring tool that can help detect attacks. Although it's not technically considered an intrusion detection system, antivirus software has become a necessary tool for preventing cybersecurity incidents.

The antivirus software market is filled with vendors, each with its unique advantages and disadvantages. It's worthwhile to analyze each vendor's offerings to see what specific features best fit your situation.

In its *Guide to Malware Incident Prevention and Handling for Desktops and Laptops* (NIST Special Publication 800-83 Revision 1), NIST recommends that antivirus solutions have the following capabilities:

- Scanning critical host components such as startup files and boot records.
- Watching real-time activities on hosts to check for suspicious activity, such as scanning e-mail and e-mail attachments for malware.
- Monitoring the behavior of typical applications such as e-mail clients, web browsers, and instant messaging software, particularly for those applications likely to be conduits for malware.
- Scanning files for known malware, including all hard drive scanning and user-initiated scans.
- Disinfecting files, which refers to removing malware from within a file.
- Quarantining files, which means that files containing malware are stored in isolation for future disinfection or examination.
- Identifying common types of malware as well as attacker tools.

NIST also recommends that organizations deploy antivirus software that uses both host- and network-based scanning. Finally, NIST recommends that organizations use centrally managed antivirus software controlled and monitored regularly by antivirus administrators responsible for its acquisition, updating, and testing throughout the organization.

You can experience conflicts between your antivirus software and some of your vendors' software. Make sure you continue scanning data files and USB files in particular. Try resolving conflicts between your antivirus system and the vendors' software by avoiding scans of core application files or database files.

3. **Deploy One or More Centralized Log File Monitors and Configure Logging Devices throughout the Organization to Send Data Back to the Centralized Log Monitor**
   (DE.AE-3: Event data are aggregated and correlated from multiple sources and sensors.)

As each event in a system occurs, the intrusion detection system stores data surrounding that event, reviews each log event, and looks for patterns associated with an intrusion or attack. While an individual intrusion detection system can look at only one system, a log file monitor can examine data across multiple systems.

Information regarding an incident might end up recorded in several places, such as firewalls, routers, network IDPSs (intrusion detection and protection systems), host IDPSs, and application logs. For the intrusion detection (and prevention) system to work, it's crucial to create a centralized log file.

A log file monitor can look at multiple logs from different systems. Make sure to configure all your systems and devices to send data back to the log file monitor. These systems are commonly referred to as security information and event management or SIEMs.

A recent shift in vendor solutions and practitioners' usage has embraced user and entity behavior analytics (UEBA). These systems bring more analytics capabilities into the storage systems than SIEMs that store logs and use prewritten correlation rules to produce alerts. With more data flowing from devices and attacks increasing, you should seek solutions that create high fidelity on alerts over those that merely ingest and change logs.

Relevant Technical Standards for DE.AE-3

Event data are collected and correlated from multiple sources and sensors

- CIS CSC 1, 3, 4, 5, 6, 7, 8, 11, 12, 13, 14, 15, 16
- COBIT 5 BAI08.02
- ISA 62443-3-3:2013 SR 6.1
- ISO/IEC 27001:2013 A.12.4.1, A.16.1.7
- NIST SP 800-53 Rev. 4 AU-6, CA-7, IR-4, IR-5, IR-8, SI-4

---

4. **Determine the Impact of Events Both Before and After they Occur**
   (DE.AE-4: Impact of events is determined.)

Be proactive in determining events before they happen, a task that is made easier based on your organization's risk assessment scenarios. However, you cannot gauge all events in advance, even though most IT and security specialists have some sense of the risks they face.

You can document many common attacks and required reactions into your organizational incident response plan. Thinking this through beforehand and agreeing on appropriate steps will allow for a much cleaner response effort.

Anytime you can identify a potential incident, you should include it in the incident response plan.

For events that come as a total surprise, assess the impact after it happens. Once the dust has settled, and the incident is fully contained, capture the lessons learned in the response plans. The sooner you can capture this in the response plan, the better the information will be for use in future response activities.

Relevant Technical Standards for DE.AE-4

Impact of events is determined

- CIS CSC 4, 6
- COBIT 5 APO12.06, DSS03.01
- ISO/IEC 27001:2013 A.16.1.4
- NIST SP 800-53 Rev. 4 CP-2, IR-4, RA-3, SI-4

---

5. Develop a Threshold for How Many Times an Event Can Occur Before You Take Action
(DE.AE-5: Incident alert thresholds are established.)

Establish thresholds about when to trigger incident alerts or actions taken in response to incident alerts. For example, one anomaly might not trigger an incident alert, but three anomalies within a specified time frame might. (Using the bank example, one major purchase might not trigger an alert, but three purchases in an hour from unusual locations might.) You can also use thresholds to determine privileges for access to system assets (e.g., three consecutive failed admin logins might trigger an alert.). These thresholds should be governed, reviewed, and adjusted over time while learning more about the baseline of activity established under DE.AE-1 described earlier. Use the detection processes to inform other detection and protection capabilities cyclically.

Relevant Technical Standards for DE.AE-5

Incident alert thresholds are established

- CIS CSC 6, 19
- COBIT 5 APO12.06, DSS03.01
- ISA 62443-2-1:2009 4.2.3.10
- ISO/IEC 27001:2013 A.16.1.4
- NIST SP 800-53 Rev. 4 IR-4, IR-5, IR-8

B. Continuous Monitoring

Given the highly complex nexus of software, the internet, and IP-based connected hardware, it's impossible to prevent security attacks. That's why the best solution is to detect attacks as soon as possible.

Voices of Experience
On Continuous Monitoring

Continuous Monitoring Needs to Actually Be Continuous

The continuous monitoring category controls I have found over and over again, is once you start the process, you don't stop. You must explain to leadership that, you do not pay for this once and you are done. This is a continuous program you must manage and mature.

Continuous Monitoring Needs a Business Case

Which sources do I need to monitor that give me the visibility picture I need? We can monitor anything and pull logs, but it needs to make business sense. We need to own what is generating the logs and it should not be owned by a third party. As you pull those logs in, you need to determine what to do with them. The hardest part here are the discussions around if it's to be a long-term metric that you're going to be collecting and want to be able to measure overtime in order to know if things get better. Or is it a metric that every quarter you want to know how many incidents you have with a group of people or specific data source? You need to determine if collecting the data will be used to protect an asset or reduce a risk, just to collect the data.

Gary Hayslip, CISO, Softbank

Periodic assessments are therefore not as efficient as continuous monitoring of systems and assets. Continuous monitoring means uninterrupted monitoring, even if you only collect data at discrete intervals.

While it may not be desirable or practical to monitor everything, at a minimum, you should continuously monitor the systems designated by your organization's risk assessment as most critical.

This section of the chapter will walk you through strategies for developing continuous monitoring that is optimal for detecting attacks as quickly as possible.

1. **Develop Strategies for Detecting Breaches as Soon as Possible, Emphasizing Continuous Surveillance of Systems through Network Monitoring**
   (DE.CM-1: The network is monitored to detect potential cybersecurity events.)

Because attackers can gain entry into networks and systems from a growing array of vectors, using a wide variety of existing and emerging attack tools, you should develop strategies for detecting breaches as soon as possible. These strategies should take into account all the various openings through which attackers can slide.

Network and host-based monitoring solutions, such as EDR (endpoint detection and response) that oversee systems' operations via various software tools, are essential in detecting and reporting many assets' failures. These systems will measure CPU utilization, network bandwidth, and other aspects of operations and send out messages over the network to check if operations are normal. These monitoring solutions should also send out alerts to designated destinations (e-mails, servers, or phones) to notify about anomalies.

There are built-in functions with applications that allow you to monitor devices on the network. One to start with is a traffic analyzer, either virtual or physical. Connecting a laptop or server to ingest network traffic into a security monitoring solution can be a good start.

There are also several open-source and free software solutions available. One solution that stands out for many administrators to begin network monitoring with is Security Onion. Security Onion is an open-source Linux distribution purpose built for threat hunting, enterprise security monitoring, and log management. It includes Elasticsearch, Logstash, Kibana, Snort, Suricata, Bro/Zeek, Wazuh, Sguil, Squert, NetworkMiner, and many other security tools.

There are many network monitoring solutions to choose from, and it's vital to pick the right one based on your risk assessment, configuration, and strategies for detecting breaches.

Relevant Technical Standards for DE.CM-1

The network is monitored to detect potential cybersecurity events

- CIS CSC 1, 7, 8, 12, 13, 15, 16
- COBIT 5 DSS01.03, DSS03.05, DSS05.07
- ISA 62443-3-3:2013 SR 6.2
- NIST SP 800-53 Rev. 4 AC-2, AU-12, CA-7, CM-3, SC-5, SC-7, SI-4

---

2. **Ensure That Appropriate Access to the Physical Environment Is Monitored, Most Likely through Electronic Monitoring or Alarm Systems**
   (DE.CM-2: The physical environment is monitored to detect potential cybersecurity events.)

Although it may not always be obvious, monitoring systems and assets' physical environment is a crucial part of cybersecurity. You can accomplish this physical monitoring in a variety of ways. Most organizations choose electronic monitoring through video cameras connected to recording equipment and closed-circuit TV systems. This method, however, requires human capital in the form of someone watching the video on a 24/7 basis to stop a cyberattack effectively and is most often used in forensic investigations following an attack.

Another method is to put critical assets in locations wired by alarm systems that rely on motion detectors, glass breakage detectors, or contact sensors.

You should correlate physical access data with network or IT access data. One scenario that proves itself is in identifying superhuman travel. As an example, you could monitor VPN access and door access to a campus. Suppose you monitor the logs to alert when those two activities happen within a short space of time. In that case, you could investigate if the user was physically in the building or accessing remotely from home.

> ## Relevant Technical Standards for DE.CM-2
>
> **The physical environment is monitored to detect potential cybersecurity events**
>
> - CIS CSC 5, 7, 14, 16
> - COBIT 5 DSS05.07
> - ISA 62443-3-3:2013 SR 6.2
> - ISO/IEC 27001:2013 A.12.4.1, A.12.4.3
> - NIST SP 800-53 Rev. 4 AC-2, AU-12, AU-13, CA-7, CM-10, CM-11

3. Monitor Employee Behavior in Terms of Both Physical and Electronic Access to Detect Unauthorized Access

(DE.CM-3: Personnel activity is monitored to detect potential cybersecurity threats.)

Maintaining a cybersecurity culture means ensuring that employees abide by the security protocols and processes in place. Most cyber incidents stem from misuse or abuse of employee-granted accounts. By monitoring user behavior and tying it to actual humans, you can determine whether the activity is legitimate.

For example, some analytics platforms can determine a baseline for typing speeds of individuals or common access folders. Once a user departs from their established baseline, an alert can fire for investigation. You can assess several behaviors this way, such as logon times, logon locations, attempts to access deactivated or suspended accounts, repeated attempts to use administrative privileges, or even the amount of data saved locally.

Therefore, you should establish methods that monitor employees' physical and electronic access to systems and document who gains access to facilities and digital assets.

> ## Relevant Technical Standards for DE.CM-3
>
> **Personnel activity is monitored to detect potential cybersecurity events**
>
> - CIS CSC 5, 7, 14, 16
> - COBIT 5 DSS05.07
> - ISA 62443-3-3:2013 SR 6.2
> - ISO/IEC 27001:2013 A.12.4.1, A.12.4.3
> - NIST SP 800-53 Rev. 4 AC-2, AU-12, AU-13, CA-7, CM-10, CM-11

4. Develop a System for Ensuring That Software Is Free of Malicious Code through Software Code Inspection and Vulnerability Assessments

(DE.CM-4: Malicious code is detected.)

Malicious code performs unauthorized functions and causes normal systems operations to become abnormal (e.g., viruses, worms, Trojans, programming flaws, etc.). Therefore, it's essential to develop systems that check for malicious code in software through various means, including code inspection, independent vulnerability assessments, code compare tools, and more. Ensure that all free software or shareware used in the development process has been certified as free of malicious code.

Relevant Technical Standards for DE.CM-4

Malicious code is detected

- CIS CSC 4, 7, 8, 12
- COBIT 5 DSS05.01
- ISA 62443-2-1:2009 4.3.4.3.8
- ISA 62443-3-3:2013 SR 3.2
- ISO/IEC 27001:2013 A.12.2.1
- NIST SP 800-53 Rev. 4 SI-3, SI-8

---

5. **Monitor Mobile Code Applications (e.g., Java Applets) for Malicious Activity by Authenticating the Codes' Origins, Verifying their Integrity, and Limiting the Actions they Can Perform**
(DE.CM-5: Unauthorized mobile code is detected.)

Mobile code, such as Java applets, ActiveX, Flash, and a host of intelligent agents, can be executed on one or more hosts other than those for which they were developed. Mobile code is prevalent and versatile, but it is also highly vulnerable to malicious intrusion. Mobile code often attaches to widely used software and frequently requires the download of a plug-in.

Because mobile code has different origins and identities from the software to which it's attached, you should identify and authenticate the code's sources. Moreover, you should scan mobile code for integrity, and any actions it performs must be limited through access control or checked through verification controls.

Relevant Technical Standards for DE.CM-5

Unauthorized mobile code is detected

- CIS CSC 7, 8
- COBIT 5 DSS05.01
- ISA 62443-3-3:2013 SR 2.4
- ISO/IEC 27001:2013 A.12.5.1, A.12.6.2
- NIST SP 800-53 Rev. 4 SC-18, SI-4, SC-44

---

6. **Evaluate a Provider's Internal and External Controls' Adequacy and Ensure they Develop and Adhere to Appropriate Policies, Procedures, and Standards; Consider the Results of Internal and External Audits**
(DE.CM-6: External service provider activity is monitored to detect potential cybersecurity events.)

One problem facing security professionals is the lack of control over the security practices of key service providers. An organization can have the best security controls and processes in place, but they are highly compromised if a critical service provider has lax security controls or standards.

Therefore, it's important to establish methods for evaluating an external provider's security controls' adequacy and to ensure they adhere to your organization's policies, procedures, and standards. Examine any internal or external security audits the provider has available and check in with peers and user groups to gauge whether the provider meets your organization's standards.

In cases where vendors need remote support, consider giving those vendors some VPN access (preferably through a proxy device) so that they are not at the core of your network. Or offer them remote access that doesn't expose your sensitive network operations to unnecessary risk. As a start to addressing this control, apply the same or as many as possible controls from monitoring internal systems and employees to your service providers.

Relevant Technical Standards for DE.CM-6

External service provider activity is monitored to detect potential cybersecurity events

- COBIT 5 APO07.06, APO10.05
- ISO/IEC 27001:2013 A.14.2.7, A.15.2.1
- NIST SP 800-53 Rev. 4 CA-7, PS-7, SA-4, SA-9, SI-4

---

7. **Monitor Employee Activity for Security Purposes and Assess When Unauthorized Access Occurs**
   (DE.CM-7: Monitoring for unauthorized personnel, connections, devices, and software is performed.)

Consider using employee monitoring software for security purposes. However, this monitoring activity may cause concern among employees; you are well-advised to implement this monitoring with great care.

Most IT and cybersecurity professionals have little interest in knowing what employees do outside the security context and typically have no desire to enforce management's organizational productivity goals. Instead, the purpose of using employee monitoring software is to limit employee actions, often unintentional, that might harm the organization's security posture.

Relevant Technical Standards for DE.CM-7

Monitoring for unauthorized personnel, connections, devices, and software is performed

- CIS CSC 1, 2, 3, 5, 9, 12, 13, 15, 16
- COBIT 5 DSS05.02, DSS05.05
- ISO/IEC 27001:2013 A.12.4.1, A.14.2.7, A.15.2.1
- NIST SP 800-53 Rev. 4 AU-12, CA-7, CM-3, CM-8, PE-3, PE-6, PE-20, SI-4

8. Use Vulnerability Scanning Tools to Find Your Organization's Weaknesses

(DE.CM-8: Vulnerability scans are performed.)

Vulnerability scanning tools hunt for weaknesses in systems and networks, and cybercriminals use them frequently to find holes that exploit your organization's digital assets. Their goal is to find devices that are open to known vulnerabilities.

Therefore, organizations should consider using vulnerability scanning tools to search for devices on the network that are open to vulnerabilities before attackers can take advantage of those flaws. These tools will primarily hunt for devices that need patching and, if run thoroughly, can be intrusive and even cause machines to crash.

Be careful in balancing your network and systems' stability against a thorough enough vulnerability scan, which you should run on a regular schedule to ensure protection. While many organizations run vulnerability scans quarterly or only twice a year, a well-built vulnerability management program will scan more frequently. It would help if you attempted to scan after you deploy bug fixes, code changes, or patches. These post-change scans will allow you to identify assets that fixes didn't install correctly. It will also allow significantly more time for the production support teams in IT and OT to develop a plan to patch found vulnerabilities.

Be careful when only identifying vulnerabilities and not taking appropriate remediation steps. If you scan and find issues but take no action, your organization might be responsible if an attacker exploits it and it's made public.

Another risk to manage is the vulnerability scanning platform's security. Effective solutions will require some elevated credentials to scan systems in your environment thoroughly. Be very diligent in securing the accounts the vulnerability scanning platform uses and keeping them patched and updated. Attackers sometimes target these systems to gain further access into an organization.

Relevant Technical Standards for DE.CM-8

Vulnerability scans are performed

- CIS CSC 1, 2, 3, 5, 9, 12, 13, 15, 16
- CIS CSC 4, 20
- COBIT 5 BAI03.10, DSS05.01
- ISO/IEC 27001:2013 A.12.6.1
- NIST SP 800-53 Rev. 4 RA-5

C.   Detection Processes

Cybersecurity monitoring processes deal with internal management and personnel structures of how cybersecurity incidents are detected and the adoption of policies that support threat detection. Cybersecurity detection processes are a series of practices related to planning, implementing, managing, and testing the policies that support these activities.

These processes track the identification of people who access resources and protect private information – establishing these kinds of methods and policies helps with a forensic examination and enhances detection functions. In some industries, they are even a matter of regulatory compliance. Outside of regulated industries, detection processes apply primarily to large organizations.

The challenges to establishing detection processes in any organization include:

- understanding the need to secure the entire network environment from internal and external threats,
- designing effective security monitoring,
- providing an overall picture of the organization's security efforts for remediation purposes,
- maintaining policies and practices that correlate security reports with established policies to ease efforts in detecting suspicious activities,
- enforcing security monitoring while balancing business needs, and
- determining acceptable risk levels.

In the next section of this chapter, we'll walk you through some critical factors you need to know to establish your organization's detection processes.

1. **Establish a Clear Delineation between Network and Security Detection, with the Networking Group and the Security Group Having Distinct and Different Responsibilities**
   (DE.DP-1: Roles and responsibilities for detection are well defined to ensure accountability.)

If your organization is large enough, split networking and security detection functions between two separate teams, with each team ideally having a different chain of command. Networking involves keeping resources up and available. Security detection is about monitoring the system for abnormalities. In many cases, network administrators rate network concerns as more important than security concerns and can override legitimate concerns about security threats.

If you work in a small operation where you can't split the delineation of functions among multiple individuals, you should consider brainstorming methods for allocating network and security functions among a few trusted individuals.

Relevant Technical Standards for DE.DP-1

Roles and responsibilities for detection are well defined to ensure accountability

- CIS CSC 19
- COBIT 5 APO01.02, DSS05.01, DSS06.03
- ISA 62443-2-1:2009 4.4.3.1
- ISO/IEC 27001:2013 A.6.1.1, A.7.2.2
- NIST SP 800-53 Rev. 4 CA-2, CA-7, PM-14

2. **Create a Formal Detection Oversight and Control Management Function; Define Leadership for a Security Review, Operational Roles, and a Formal Organizational Plan; Train Reviewers to Perform Their Duties Correctly and Implement the Review Process**

(DE.DP-2: Detection activities comply with applicable requirements.)

To ensure that your detection activities align with your organization's business goals, operating philosophies, legal requirements, and contractual obligations, you should establish mechanisms for oversight and control. Include this as part of your established governance and risk programs by making it a standing agenda item for discussion. Where possible, bring in other parties to this: HR, legal, procurement, IT, internal audit, and business line leadership. These groups represent those with a vested interest in addressing risks identified or discussed as part of detection activities.

For larger organizations, it is helpful to create a formal detection oversight and control management function, which entails the following:

- **Initiation**: Define the leadership for security review, operational roles, and a formal organizational plan.
- **Identify relevant review issues**: Identify and prioritize the key issues.
- **Create a generic review plan**: Define all pertinent audit and control activities.
- **Deploy the procedures to guide the review process**: Train reviewers in the necessary steps for conducting reviews.
- **Implement the review process**: Assign roles and responsibilities, develop schedules, define and perform monitoring activities, and report and resolve problems.

For smaller organizations, you should consider brainstorming ways to create formal detection oversight and control management functions for those trusted individuals who already wear multiple hats and play various roles.

These reviews should provide sufficient documentation that the detection processes are in place and comply with organizational, legal, and regulatory requirements. If you identify problems during the review, you should address them before the review can continue.

Review reports should be made available to managers by easily accessible means. Since the outcome of these review processes contains valuable information about your detection processes, it's essential to keep a record of how you conducted the review.

Relevant Technical Standards for DE.DP-2

Detection activities comply with all applicable requirements

- COBIT 5 DSS06.01, MEA03.03, MEA03.04
- ISA 62443-2-1:2009 4.4.3.2
- ISO/IEC 27001:2013 A.18.1.4, A.18.2.2, A.18.2.3
- NIST SP 800-53 Rev. 4 AC-25, CA-2, CA-7, SA-18, SI-4, PM-14

3. Test Detection Processes Either Manually or in an Automated Fashion in Conformance with the Organization's Risk Assessment
(DE.DP-3: Detection processes are tested.)

Once you've created your detection process, test each activity for conformance to risk requirements. This testing will make sure that you've implemented the security control properly. One way to test each activity is to use a management tool called a "process requirements testing matrix," which has two parts. One part manages the life cycle of the process requirement, while the other manages process activities.

You can establish tests either through manual or automated processes. In a manual process, an evaluator will manually test the process. Using the banking example, an evaluator might manually try to force a transaction that the system should reject. Automated methods perform the same functions, except using a computerized process (having a program, for example, trying to force a prohibited transaction).

Use your yearly or regularly conducted external penetration test exercises or engagements to test your detection processes. These can be very informative and are made to simulate an actual attack. To truly test your detection processes and, more importantly, your team, do not announce that the "attack" is from the authorized penetration test, which is a fruitful way to tabletop or exercise your plans and previous training.

Relevant Technical Standards for DE.DP-3

Detection processes are tested

- COBIT 5 APO13.02, DSS05.02
- ISA 62443-2-1:2009 4.4.3.2
- ISA 62443-3-3:2013 SR 3.3
- ISO/IEC 27001:2013 A.14.2.8
- NIST SP 800-53 Rev. 4 CA-2, CA-7, PE-3, SI-3, SI-4, PM-14

---

4. Inform Relevant Personnel Who Must Use Data or Network Security Information about What Is Happening and Otherwise Facilitate Organizational Communication
(DE.DP-4: Event detection information is communicated to appropriate parties.)

Event detection reporting is the goal of these processes and is critical to uncovering malicious events. Event reports show where vulnerabilities exist so that you can remediate them. It is crucial to inform relevant personnel about event detection results so that remediation occurs in an informed and effective manner.

Event detection reporting is an effective means of ensuring that security personnel can stay informed of security issues at all organizational levels. It also facilitates improved administrative communications by distributing information about security throughout the organization. Any detection information should have a pathway toward your written incident response plan. You can use these data to mature the plan's overall effectiveness and inform your organization of gaps in your process.

Relevant Technical Standards for DE.DP-4

Event detection information is communicated

- CIS CSC 19
- COBIT 5 APO08.04, APO12.06, DSS02.05
- ISA 62443-2-1:2009 4.3.4.5.9
- ISA 62443-3-3:2013 SR 6.1
- ISO/IEC 27001:2013 A.16.1.2, A.16.1.3
- NIST SP 800-53 Rev. 4 AU-6, CA-2, CA-7, RA-5, SI-4

---

5. **Document the Process for Event Detection to Improve the Organization's Detection Systems**
(DE.DP-5: Detection processes are continuously improved.)

When it comes to critical events, most organizations respond reactively and focus on getting back to business as soon as possible. To prevent future occurrences and gain further insight into your organization's security posture, you should develop records and analysis that delivers insight into why the event happened and how to prevent a similar occurrence in the future.

You should, therefore, document processes for detecting events, both during and after the events. Use that information to improve the organization's operations and systems for detecting, investigating, and limiting future incidents' damage. Develop metrics that feed into key performance indicators (KPIs) relevant to the business.

Relevant Technical Standards for DE.DP-5

Detection processes are continuously improved

- COBIT 5 APO11.06, APO12.06, DSS04.05
- ISA 62443-2-1:2009 4.4.3.4
- ISO/IEC 27001:2013 A.16.1.6
- NIST SP 800-53 Rev. 4 CA-2, CA-7, PL-2, RA-5, SI-4, PM-14

SUMMARY

Based on the practical applications of the NIST Framework that we've presented in this chapter, here are the critical take-aways regarding the tools and techniques for detecting a cyberattack:

- Detecting a cyber incident among thousands or millions of routine changes across systems has become increasingly challenging.
- Adding to the challenges of detecting incidents are the techniques that malicious actors use to hide their tracks.

- The Detect function in the NIST Framework focuses on spotting when anomalies and events occur in your system.
- Before you can detect anomalies, you must establish "normal" baselines.
- You can learn about events using intrusion detection systems.
- Antivirus software is a crucial monitoring tool that can help prevent cybersecurity events.
- You will find it helpful to deploy a centralized log file that looks across multiple logs across different systems.
- It would help if you considered trying to gauge the impact of events before and after they occur based on your organization's risk assessment.
- You will find it helpful to set thresholds on how often an event occurs before you flag it as abnormal.
- It would help if you considered continuously monitoring systems designated by your organization's risk assessment as most critical.
- It would help if you tried, to the extent possible, to monitor appropriate access to your systems' physical environments.
- You should consider establishing methods that monitor employees' physical and electronic access to systems and document who gains access to facilities and digital assets.
- You should consider developing systems that check for malicious code in software through a variety of means.
- You should consider identifying and authenticating the origins and identity of mobile code.
- It would help if you considered establishing methods for evaluating an external provider's security controls' adequacy to ensure they adhere to your organization's policies, procedures, and standards.
- You should *very carefully* consider using employee monitoring software for security purposes.
- It would help if you considered using vulnerability scanning tools to search for devices on the network that are open to vulnerabilities.
- Establishing your organization's detection processes can be complicated but it is extremely helpful in understanding what's happening in your network and effectively monitoring security.
- Large organizations should consider splitting their networking and security detection functions.
- Large organizations should consider creating a formal detection oversight and control management function.
- Make sure you test your detection systems either manually or through automated functions.
- Make sure you inform relevant personnel about detection operations.
- Make sure you document event detection to improve your detection systems in the future.

CHAPTER QUIZ

Take this quick quiz to learn about how to manage cyberattacks. The answers are given at the end of the book.

1. **What is the first step in detecting anomalies that may indicate a cyberattack? (Select one.)**
   a. Develop a process within your organization for handling attacks and incidents.
   b. Install an intrusion detection system.
   c. Establish baselines for determining what "normal" is and what is "abnormal."
2. **Which of the following are some of the challenges in establishing an intrusion detection system? (Select all that apply.)**
   a. Staff may decide that some incidents that are alerted through the intrusion detection system aren't problems.
   b. Networks must continue to operate while intrusion detection systems run.
   c. Intrusion detection systems often issue misleading messages.
3. **If your organization can't establish network monitoring solutions for all systems and assets, which of the following should you do? (Select one.)**
   a. Rely on your intrusion detection systems to catch cyberattacks.
   b. Run network monitoring solutions on those assets designated in your organization's risk assessment to be the most critical.
   c. Make sure to deploy antivirus systems that use host-based as well as network-based scanning.
4. **Which of the following are some of the key benefits of establishing detection processes? (Select all that apply.)**
   a. The event reports generated from these processes can yield insight into avoiding malicious attacks in the future.
   b. Event reporting that occurs under detection processes helps keep relevant personnel informed and foster better organizational communication.
   c. Detection processes help us evaluate the adequacy of providers' security practices.

ESSENTIAL READING FOR TOOLS AND TECHNIQUES FOR DETECTING A CYBERATTACK

M. Hathaway, ed., *Best Practices in Computer Network Defense: Incident Detection and Response* (IOS Press, 2014).

Nikolaos Pitropaki, Emmanouil Panaousis, Alkiviadis Giannakoulias, George Kalpakis, Rodrigo Diaz Rodriguez, and Panayiotis Sarigiannidis, An Enhanced Cyber Attack Attribution FramChapter work, *International Conference on Trust and Privacy in Digital Business*, 213–228.

R. Brewer, Cyber threats: reducing the time to detection and response, *Network Security*, May 2015 at https://www.sciencedirect.com/science/article/abs/pii/S1353485815300374.

Developing a Continuity of Operations Plan

Overview of Chapter and Objective

This chapter will provide the reader with fundamental concepts and practical steps to respond to and recover from a cybersecurity incident. By the end of this chapter, the reader will grasp the concepts necessary to develop an incident response plan (IRP), maintaining communications within the response team and the broader organization throughout an incident. The chapter will introduce the reader to the basic concepts of how to contain and mitigate an incident. Finally, the chapter will introduce the reader to the basic principles and elements of developing a recovery plan and the importance of lessons learned in the aftermath of a cybersecurity incident.

Melinda just got home from an awards dinner and checked her e-mail for the first time that night. As CEO, Melinda always faced a full inbox no matter how many times she checked her messages. Mixed in with regular e-mails was a very odd one from an address unfamiliar to Melinda.

"We have hacked your computer systems. Prepare to suffer, fools!" was the subject line of the strange message.

Although she was afraid to open the e-mail, she did.

In the body of the e-mail, the sender wrote, "Your network is hacked! We have six terabytes of data." Embedded in the e-mail and attached to it was proof that whoever sent the e-mail had internal code development files and so much more.

Cybersecurity Risk Management: Mastering the Fundamentals Using the NIST Cybersecurity Framework, First Edition. Cynthia Brumfield and Brian Haugli.
© 2022 Cynthia Brumfield and Brian Haugli. Published 2022 by John Wiley & Sons, Inc.

Melinda immediately called her general counsel John, who was napping in his hotel room in Hong Kong. John asked Melinda to forward the e-mail to him, and he would review it and get back to her. "No one else should know for now," Melinda ordered.

Two hours later, John called Melinda back and told her that the situation appeared dire. From the looks of it, the e-mail sender actually had stolen a wealth of internal files, staff e-mails, and code, including the source code for the company's proprietary recommendation engine, which accounted for 40% of the network's profit.

John advised Melinda to share the e-mail with the network's chief operating officer, Anand. Melinda agreed but told John that no one aside from Anand should know.

Anand wanted to share the e-mail with his chief security officer, Susan, and have her team investigate the situation. He had to wait for six hours while Melinda and John both caught some sleep and then brainstormed the problem until John authorized him to let Susan launch an investigation.

Before Susan and her technical team could get far into the investigation, Melinda received a ransom e-mail from the same person asking for $15 million in bitcoin, or else, he said, he would release all the materials on the internet. John urged Melinda to contact the FBI, but Melinda was hesitant to stir up any negative publicity until she understood what was going on. Let's examine our options for just a bit, and let's keep a lid on who knows about this situation, Melinda told John and Anand.

Meanwhile, Susan's team was frantic – nobody knew what was going on or what they needed to examine. All they knew was the company had been hacked and they had to find out what happened. After many confusing and conflicting directives from Susan, someone on the team discovered there had been a massive exfiltration of files – nearly six terabytes worth of data.

Just as Susan began to report the massive data theft back to Anand, Melinda received another e-mail. This time the attacker said that he would not only start releasing files on the internet, but he would also begin deleting company files if he did not receive the ransom within 12 hours. Melinda then conferenced with John, Anand, and Susan. All agreed they should contact the FBI.

Just as the team assembled at headquarters to meet with FBI specialists, every company employee's computer screen displayed a message from the attacker. The bad actor warned them that their bosses weren't playing ball and that he would wipe their computers within 10 hours. The hacker was still inside the network. At that point, a local newspaper got a hold of the hacker's message and posted a piece about it on the paper's website.

Melinda's phone was ringing off the hook with calls from angry board members who saw the article. All she could tell them was that the hacker had stolen many files and was demanding $15 million, and her ad hoc team was working with the FBI.

An hour after the FBI began its work, a mysterious website appeared that featured a selection of embarrassing internal e-mails and selected bits of the proprietary code. The message on the site spelled out that the hacker had everything and would release it all unless he got paid by the deadline.

Wall Street noticed, and the company's stock started to tank. Someone on Susan's team found the hacker's point of entry, a backdoor in an unpatched piece of server software, and shut down the threat of any files getting deleted. But that was the only bright spot. Melinda didn't pay the ransom under advice from the FBI, and the hacker dumped all the stolen files.

Ten months later, the Justice Department brought multiple computer fraud, theft, and extortion charges against a former Russian military hacker operating out of a ransomware ring. Melinda, John, Anand, and Susan were forced to resign from the company months before that.

INTRODUCTION

As the situation at Melinda's company illustrates, the steps you take after discovering a cybersecurity incident are critical to any organization's success. Recovering from a cyberattack or other adverse cybersecurity incident can take days, weeks, or even months. Recovering from a bad reputation earned by a mismanaged cyberattack can take years.

That's why it's crucial to design comprehensive business continuity and disaster recovery plans that can limit the damage and shorten the recovery window. Taking the time to map out an effective continuity and recovery plan will be well worth your while and benefit your organization's long-term health and functioning.

The two central pillars of developing a continuity of operations plan are response and recovery, the two main topics we will walk you through in the following sections.

A.   ONE SIZE DOES NOT FIT ALL

As is true of every chapter in this book, this chapter is aimed at all organizations while recognizing that each organization is unique. Some of the concepts we present may be very applicable to your situation, but some may not be. Everything in cybersecurity is contingent on specifics, with no one-size-fits-all solution. Depending on your organization's size, assets, configuration, and budgets, some of the principles we discuss may be precisely what you need or only partially relevant right now or very important to plans, or not relevant at all.

We highly recommend that you delve into technical resources, primarily standards, that we present at the end of each significant section for those who have the time and resources. This chapter provides a high-level view of the topics covered to introduce you to some basic cybersecurity concepts. The technical resources listed at the end of each section will deliver the nitty-gritty of technically accomplishing each of the concepts discussed.

I.   RESPONSE

Response to an unwanted cybersecurity incident is most commonly known as incident response. Incident response is an organized plan for addressing and managing the aftermath of an attack or breach, or compromise. This plan should have a policy that helps you define what an incident is in the first place and should contain a critical definition or set of definitions that will trigger all the other activities within the response plan.

These definitions will be contingent on your specific circumstances. The critical thing to remember is that the ultimate goal of incident response is to limit damage and reduce recovery time and costs when an adverse cyber incident affects your organization.

To most effectively respond to an incident, organizations should have an established computer security incident response team, or CSIRT, including personnel from across the organization, such as legal, human resources, and public relations professionals. The most practical first step is to scan your organization and decide which personnel would be most useful on this CSIRT, regardless of your organization's size or simplicity. Even small organizations should designate multiple personnel to be on the CSIRT to gain as diverse input as possible.

Your first instinct might be to rely primarily on technical personnel to develop your suggested CSIRT members to emphasize and quickly implement technical responses to the incident. However, involving top management and maintaining internal and external organizational communication across various job functions should be considered on par with technical solutions for successful incident response and recovery.

Let one recent real-world example of inadequate incident response, which was poorly organized, ill-timed, and badly managed, be an object lesson in the importance of establishing a good plan and a good incident response team. Credit rating agency Equifax experienced a massive data breach that exposed sensitive data on 143 million Americans.

In the aftermath of the public revelation of that breach, Equifax quickly posted a website for consumers that

- contained security vulnerabilities,
- required consumers to waive any rights to sue the company,
- used an odd-looking domain name that raised the suspicions of both consumers and security professionals,
- asked nervous consumers to input sensitive data such as the last four digits of their social security numbers,
- told consumers to pay if they wanted to freeze credit checks in the wake of the breach, and
- directed some consumers via Twitter to an actual phishing site.

Perhaps worst of all, Equifax waited at least six weeks to inform anyone of the breach, during which time one executive aware of the breach sold company stock and was later charged by the SEC for insider trading. The upshot of Equifax's incident response missteps was the quick departure of its CEO, CIO, and CTO, public condemnation, congressional inquiries, threatened legislation, and ongoing government investigations.

With a proper incident response plan and a well-organized CSIRT, these negative repercussions could have been, if not avoided, then reduced to more manageable situations.

In this next section, we'll walk you through some steps you can take to get closer to effective incident response. These steps will help you:

- Develop an executable response plan.
- Understand the importance of communications in incident response.
- Prepare for corporate-wide involvement in incident response.

A. Develop an Executable Response Plan
(RS.RP-1: Response plan is executed during or after an event.)

The NIST Cybersecurity Framework defines the outcome of an incident response plan as "response processes and procedures are executed and maintained, to ensure timely response to detected cybersecurity events."

This broad definition will vary from organization to organization depending on the nature of the business, its size, and the skill sets among its employees. Therefore, the first step in developing a response plan is to understand your organization's business needs and develop a plan to assign personnel various responsibilities when responding to an incident so that the plan can align to your business and human resources available. An incident response plan aims at detecting and reacting to computer security incidents, determining their scope and risk, responding appropriately to the incident, communicating the results and risk to all stakeholders, and reducing the likelihood of the incident reoccurring.

Establish Criticality for First Response: Incident response should address those most important areas of your organization first. You can determine the level of importance with an exercise of identifying either critical revenue streams or customer services and then the supporting processes, applications, and systems that enable them. Without a consensus on what's most important to your organization in an incident, it's almost impossible to implement an effective incident response.

Collaborate with Management: To understand your business needs, you must collaborate with management to hammer out commonly accepted statements that detail the steps you need to take once you detect an incident. For example, a broad, widely accepted goal might be "keep the source code protected at all times." Conversely, another commonly accepted goal might be "in the event our source code is accessed by an unauthorized third party, it's important to shut down internet-facing sites."

Create Formal Policies and Practices: Another critical step in developing an incident response plan that you can execute is the creation of formal policies and practices needed to establish your organization's incident response capabilities. A successful incident response plan cannot come from just the IT silo or technology department in your organization. It's crucial to bring the required stakeholders in during the plan's development, including representatives from the C-Suite, business teams, legal department, PR department, key outside vendors, and many other kinds of business functions. Each stakeholder should be assigned responsibilities in the event of an incident. For example, the plan might state that a top executive is responsible for authorizing any incident response actions across the organization. Or the plan might delegate that responsibility to an IT department manager who has the independent authority to send or give a member of the PR department the automatic duty of drafting a press release. It all depends on your circumstances and personnel.

Consider Insurance: A critical stakeholder that influences your success would be your insurance policy. Whenever possible, factor in the coverages, limits, and exceptions to the response plan. You may find that your current policy will cover certain costs. To maximize this, discuss in depth with your insurance broker what is or is not covered by walking through realistically probable incidents that could happen to your organization. They should be able to give you a clear understanding of what would be covered under your current policy or if you should investigate increasing your policy limits and coverage.

Test the Plan: Any plan should be thoroughly tested at least once with the goal of multiple tests via commonly accepted tabletop exercise methods. The worst action can be picking up the incident response plan for the first time when you need it.

Relevant Technical Standards for RS.RP-1

Response plan is executed during or after an incident

- CIS CSC 19
- COBIT 5 APO12.06, BAI01.10
- ISA 62443-2-1:2009 4.3.4.5.1
- ISO/IEC 27001:2013 A.16.1.5
- NIST SP 800-53 Rev. 4 CP-2, CP-10, IR-4, IR-8

Voices of Experience
On Coordinating with Stakeholders

Communicating with Peers is Powerful

My team started out fairly small compared to some of the giants of the industry. We had smart, dedicated, hardworking people. It was incredibly valuable for them to be able to collaborate with our peer companies dealing with nation-state threat actors. For instance, to get the collaboration and the sense of community that there were other people fighting the same fight. External parties with whom they could share information, get tips and tricks to enhance their skill set, but also to feel that sense of community with.

Mike Waters, former CISO, Booz Allen Hamilton

B. Understand the Importance of Communications in Incident Response

(RS.CO-1: Personnel know their roles and order of operations when a response is needed.)

Communication is perhaps the most critical incident response component, both internal communications and communications with outside stakeholders. It's crucial to make sure personnel know what they should do in responding to a cybersecurity incident. Communications in an incident response situation can be challenging. They must balance the twin objectives of openness and withholding individual pieces of information no one has corroborated or fully vetted.

When it comes to internal communications, effective communications must be in place to convey each process task in responding to the incident, with the incident response plan specifying team structures, individual roles and responsibilities, and protocols. Critical factors in the plan are when to involve executive leadership in decisions, at what threshold executives should take action, and who gets to make the decisions.

For example, the plan may call for executive leadership's immediate involvement in a situation involving financial theft. It may further specify that any theft above $1,000 requires the executive to implement the response plan. Moreover, it can state that the finance department decides when to notify the bank and that the legal department decides when to inform authorities.

Whatever incident response plan your organization develops, educational initiatives must be in place so that all affected personnel understand the plan and have the knowledge they need to fulfill their roles in it.

Relevant Technical Standards for RS.CO-1

Personnel know their roles and order of operations when a response is needed

- CIS CSC 19
- COBIT 5 EDM03.02, APO01.02, APO12.03
- ISA 62443-2-1:2009 4.3.4.5.2, 4.3.4.5.3, 4.3.4.5.4
- ISO/IEC 27001:2013 A.6.1.1, A.7.2.2, A.16.1.1
- NIST SP 800-53 Rev. 4 CP-2, CP-3, IR-3, IR-8

C. Prepare for Corporate-Wide Involvement During Some Cybersecurity Attacks

(RS.CO-4: Coordination with stakeholders occurs consistent with response plans.)

Incident response plans should include steps for communicating across the organization in some cybersecurity incidents.

Therefore, you should develop communication methods across the organization, including corporate communications, regulatory affairs, legal, compliance and audit, and business operations.

It's also essential that incident response plans include critical third parties, such as your insurance carrier, law enforcement agencies, and breach remediation and forensics experts.

Many new regulations have been introduced – for example, New York State's Department of Financial Services (NY DFS) have established a notification period for covered organizations that mandates they are notified within a certain amount of time of either a suspected or actual incident or breach. To meet these emerging regulations, an internal process must be developed to determine who is allowed to acknowledge the incident meets the criteria and then who at the governing body to contact to satisfy the notification requirement.

Relevant Technical Standards for RS.CO-4

Coordination with stakeholders occurs consistent with response plans

- CIS CSC 19
- COBIT 5 DSS03.04
- ISA 62443-2-1:2009 4.3.4.5.5
- ISO/IEC 27001:2013 Clause 7.4
- NIST SP 800-53 Rev. 4 CP-2, IR-4, IR-8

II. ANALYSIS

Once you've reported an incident, it's essential to turn to your CSIRT members to analyze it, much like law enforcement investigators begin investigating a crime. During this process, you will collect evidence, ask questions, pursue leads, and hopefully find a resolution.

At the outset, some of the questions you might ask are:

- How did the incident occur?
- When did it occur?
- Who caused the incident?
- What was damaged in the incident, and what is the extent of the damage?
- What did the perpetrators of the incident do, and what changes did they make?
- What steps should you take to ensure that the incident doesn't spread or doesn't happen again?

In the next section of the chapter, we'll walk you through some of the critical steps you can take to analyze an incident to help you achieve efficient and time-sensitive resolutions to a cybersecurity incident. These steps entail:

1. using your intrusion detection system in analyzing the incident;
2. taking steps to contain the incident;
3. eliminating or intercepting the adversary; and
4. mitigating vulnerabilities.

A. Examine Your Intrusion Detection System in Analyzing an Incident

(RS.AN-1: Notifications from detection systems are investigated.)

An analysis is a crucial component of incident response. It can indicate how the incident occurred, what systems were compromised, the extent of damage, what was taken, what changed, and how to prevent a similar incident in the future.

A critical place to start is to look at your organization's intrusion detection systems, a step that should be the very first activity of the incident response team. As discussed in an earlier chapter on detecting a cyber incident, intrusion detection systems can see incident activity, signatures, changes in files, and many more indicators that can help you analyze the attack.

This analysis could be conducted by your in-house team members or an outsourced managed security service provider (MSSP). When using an MSSP, it's essential to establish the level of notification you want to receive when alerts or notifications are fired. Too many messages can result in a less effective response overall and can become costly. Whether internal or external resources are investigated, tuning your intrusion detection systems will be required to reduce the "noise." In most cases, analysis of the intrusion detection system data can provide you with the evidence you need to resolve the situation.

Relevant Technical Standards for RS.AN-1

Notifications from detection systems are investigated

- CIS CSC 4, 6, 8, 19
- COBIT 5 DSS02.04, DSS02.07
- ISA 62443-2-1:2009 4.3.4.5.6, 4.3.4.5.7, 4.3.4.5.8
- ISA 62443-3-3:2013 SR 6.1
- ISO/IEC 27001:2013 A.12.4.1, A.12.4.3, A.16.1.5
- NIST SP 800-53 Rev. 4 AU-6, CA-7, IR-4, IR-5, PE-6, SI-4

B.   Understand the Impact of the Event
(RS.AN-2: Impact of the incident is understood.)

The incident's initial report should include some assessment of its impacts, such as the ability to access specific systems or sensitive data exposure. As the CSIRT investigates the incident, more details of the effects should become apparent. You should communicate those details to the management of the organization's functional areas affected. This communication will kick off your incident response plan built to satisfy RS.RP-1 if you haven't enacted it already. It is recommended that an incident response plan be updated after responding to major incidents that require organizational or process changes to the incident response process.

Relevant Technical Standards for RS.AN-2

The impact of the incident is understood

- COBIT 5 DSS02.02
- ISA 62443-2-1:2009 4.3.4.5.6, 4.3.4.5.7, 4.3.4.5.8
- ISO/IEC 27001:2013 A.16.1.4, A.16.1.6
- NIST SP 800-53 Rev. 4 CP-2, IR-4

C. Gather and Preserve Evidence

(RS.AN-3: Forensics are performed.)

It is vital to gather and preserve evidence that prosecutors use in pursuing computer crimes, otherwise known as digital forensics. This evidence preservation might include gathering source code, malware code, log files, monitoring files, hash values, and many other evidence sources contingent on your configuration.

Although law enforcement might ultimately use this evidence for criminal investigation, your organization's primary purpose is to help improve your cyber defenses in the future.

The information captured as evidence can give you insight into the adversary's tactics, techniques, and procedures (TTPs). These TTPs should be integrated back into your protection and detection capabilities to thwart future attacks.

Suppose you are part of an established information sharing and analytics center (ISAC). In that case, the collected evidence can be shared with others to help them identify or avoid a similar incident. In turn, being part of an ISAC allows you to gain access to this shared data to help inform your defenses.

Relevant Technical Standards for RS.AN-3

Forensics are performed

- COBIT 5 APO12.06, DSS03.02, DSS05.07
- ISA 62443-3-3:2013 SR 2.8, SR 2.9, SR 2.10, SR 2.11, SR 2.12, SR 3.9, SR 6.1
- ISO/IEC 27001:2013 A.16.1.7
- NIST SP 800-53 Rev. 4 AU-7, IR-4

D. Prioritize the Treatment of the Incident Consistent with Your Response Plan

(RS.AN-4: Incidents are categorized consistent with your response plan.)

Prioritizing the incident consistent with your response plan is the most critical element of analysis in disaster recovery. Dealing with an incident on an ad hoc basis without understanding its importance or priority could waste resources, cause further problems, and ultimately fail to help resolve the incident.

NIST's Computer Security Incident Handling Guide: SP 800-61 spells out some of the factors to consider in placing a "low," "medium," or "high" or priority on the incident. These factors are:

- **Functional impact of the incident:** Has the incident limited business functionality?
- **Informational impact of the incident:** Has the incident affected the confidentiality, integrity, or availability of the organization's information?
- **Recoverability from the incident:** What strain does the incident place on the organization's ability to recover?

Relevant Technical Standards for RS.AN-4

Incidents are categorized consistent with response plans

- CIS CSC 19
- COBIT 5 DSS02.02
- ISA 62443-2-1:2009 4.3.4.5.6
- ISO/IEC 27001:2013 A.16.1.4
- NIST SP 800-53 Rev. 4 CP-2, IR-4, IR-5, IR-8

Voices of Experience
On Vulnerability Disclosures

Bug Bounties Make You Go from Reactive to Proactive

A bug bounty program in my way of thinking is just an extension of a vulnerability disclosure program. Vulnerability disclosure has been around since the birth of the internet and one could argue well before that in terms of people just giving feedback saying "hey your door's unlocked."

What a bug bounty program does on top of that basically rewards the person who finds and reports that information with cash. And in doing so you're validating what they've done for you and you're encouraging them to do more of it and tell all their friends and all sorts of thing. And what it really does is create this extended, sort of elastic security team around your organization where people are just basically watching your back.

That's what happens when you add an incentive. It goes from being a reactive process to a proactive one.

Casey Ellis, founder, chairman and CTO of Bugcrowd

E.   Establish Processes for Handling Vulnerability Disclosures
(RS.AN-5: Processes are established to receive, analyze, and respond to vulnerabilities disclosed to the organization from internal and external sources (e.g., internal testing, security bulletins, or security researchers).)

Your organization might receive a report of a flaw in your systems or on a website, or any other technical aspect of your operations. This kind of report is called a vulnerability disclosure, or more commonly a "bug report."

Bug reports or vulnerability disclosures typically come from external sources, such as independent security researchers acting in good faith. However, they can also come from more formal information-sharing efforts such as information sharing and analysis centers (ISACs). Because these disclosures are frequently helpful means of correcting exploitable flaws in your systems and assets, it's vital to establish formal internal mechanisms for receiving, assessing, and mitigating the bugs brought to your attention.

Many of the vulnerabilities you might receive could stem not from your infrastructure and systems but also vendors' products or contractors. You should also have a process for obtaining these bug reports and passing them on to the appropriate party.

Some organizations offer outsiders incentives to find flaws in their systems, known as bug bounties, where you offer payments and legal liability protection to researchers and others to find vulnerabilities so you can fix them. You should determine if offering such incentives is a good fit for your organization.

Relevant Technical Standards for RS.AN-5

Processes are established to receive, analyze, and respond to vulnerabilities disclosed to the organization from internal and external sources (e.g., internal testing, security bulletins, or security researchers)

- CIS CSC 4, 19
- COBIT 5 EDM03.02, DSS05.07
- NIST SP 800-53 Rev. 4 SI-5, PM-15

III. MITIGATION

Once you've reported and analyzed the incident, the next step is to implement measures that prevent the incident's spread through your organization, lessening its impact. The following sections offer ideas about how to stop the spread of an incident.

A. Take Steps to Contain the Incident
(RS.MI-1: Incidents are contained.)

As incidents increase in frequency and complexity, monitoring intrusion and other systems are insufficient. As your organization begins to understand the incidents' root causes, you learn lessons that come out of investigations, leading to risk mitigation.

The first step in risk mitigation is to limit the scope and magnitude of the incident and establish procedures to contain it. Among just some of the means of managing an incident are:

- Survey the situation and determine the operational status of your networks and organizational assets.
- Isolate contaminated assets from the rest of the network and organization.
- Take forensic backups to have a record of the affected systems as they were during the incident.
- Check that your regular backup system is working in the event you need to make changes.
- Protect and keep available critical computing resources.
- Keep a low profile and avoid looking for the attacker in obvious and detectable ways.
- Avoid potentially malicious code.
- Change passwords on compromised systems and related interconnected systems.

Relevant Technical Standards for RS.MI-1

Incidents are contained

- CIS CSC 19
- COBIT 5 APO12.06
- ISA 62443-2-1:2009 4.3.4.5.6
- ISA 62443-3-3:2013 SR 5.1, SR 5.2, SR 5.4
- ISO/IEC 27001:2013 A.12.2.1, A.16.1.5
- NIST SP 800-53 Rev. 4 IR-4

B. Decrease the Threat Level by Eliminating or Intercepting the Adversary as Soon as the Incident Occurs

(RS.MI-2: Incidents are mitigated.)

You can accomplish mitigation via reducing the threat level of the incident by eliminating the threat, blocking the adversary as soon as the incident occurs, or minimizing the attack's consequences. In mitigating incidents, there are generally three acceptable strategies:

- **Acceptance:** This strategy is sound when your organization feels that the other mitigation options' cost is not worth it and the risk of the incident happening again is not very high. In other words, acceptance is a valuable strategy when the cost of avoiding the incident or limiting the incident is higher than the cost of the incident itself.
- **Avoidance:** The most expensive of mitigation options, the avoidance mitigation strategy means taking action to avoid any further exposure to the risk and is usually the most costly option in the short run.
- **Limitation:** Limitation is the most common risk strategy because it takes some action but employs some acceptance of the incident's risk.

Effective threat mitigation usually entails over time some mix of each of these three mitigation options. Professionals debate entire strategies and assessments on how to meet this control effectively. The goal is to find what works best for your organization to give you a consistent, repeatable, and cost-effective response.

Relevant Technical Standards for RS.MI-2

Incidents are mitigated

- CIS CSC 4, 19
- COBIT 5 APO12.06
- ISA 62443-2-1:2009 4.3.4.5.6, 4.3.4.5.10
- ISO/IEC 27001:2013 A.12.2.1, A.16.1.5
- NIST SP 800-53 Rev. 4 IR-4

You can break down the activity recovery as follows:

1. **Activation:** Because cyber incidents generally occur without any warning, rapid detection of the incident and quick activation of the disaster recovery program can make all the difference between a timely recovery or a protracted one. It's helpful to establish a disaster recovery committee as part of the disaster response plan and develop training for the committee members on what they should know.

   While the event is still ongoing during the activation phase, it's essential to define the event, develop notification procedures, assess the damage, and activate disaster recovery planning.

   1) **Notification Procedures:** Develop a process to alert the disaster recovery team during business and non-business hours. You should send notifications to the CSIRT to assess the damage and implement the incident response plan.

      You can undertake this notification in many ways, but some organizations benefit from a phone tree. The notification information can contain the nature of the attack, the damage caused, response and recovery details, when and where to assemble for a briefing or further response, and any other instructions about notifications.

   2) **Damage Assessment:** Disaster recovery can only begin after you conduct a damage assessment. It's vital to develop damage assessment guidelines in advance for different types of attacks based on severity and then perform the damage assessment as quickly as possible during the activation phase of recovery.

      Damage assessment procedures vary according to the nature and severity of the attack. Some factors to take into account when conducting a damage assessment might be:
      - the origin of the attack,
      - potential for additional damage,
      - areas of the system and inventory of assets affected,
      - assets that you might have to replace, and
      - estimated time frames to restore normal operations if your operations have been disrupted.

   3) **Activate Disaster Recovery Planning:** You should activate disaster recovery only after completing a complete damage assessment; otherwise, you might cause more disruptions than necessary if the damage is minimal or easily corrected.

      Make sure that your disaster recovery plan has criteria that would activate disaster recovery planning. These criteria will vary based on your specific circumstances, business goals, and a host of other factors.

      The outcome of the disaster recovery planning should be:
      - your development of a list of systems and components that you need to restore,
      - your identification of interdependencies on affected systems, with a sequence of restoration developed,
      - your estimates of time for each restoration,
      - your instructions for reporting failures to the team, and
      - your plan for communications among teams.

2. **Execution Phase:** Once you have activated the disaster recovery plan, notified staff, and assembled appropriate teams, recovery plans can begin. The focus of this phase is bringing up the disaster recovery system. Depending on the schedule, at this stage, functions could include temporary manual processing, recovery, and operation on an alternate system or relocation and recovery at an alternate site.

   - **Sequencing:** You should restore the most critical assets before less critical assets. Communicate with the disaster recovery team if you don't complete a particular activity within the expected timeframe or if it's clear you need to purchase assets before restoration.
   - **Recovery Procedures:** The disaster recovery plan should list detailed and specific step-by-step procedures for restoring assets. Among some of the standard functions that occur during this phase are:
     - getting authorization to access damaged systems,
     - notifying people that use the damaged systems,
     - obtaining and installing needed hardware,
     - obtaining and loading backup media,
     - restoring critical operating systems, software, and data,
     - testing system functions and security controls, and
     - connecting systems to network or external systems.

3. **Reconstitution and Restoration Phase:** This is the phase when you have entirely managed the disaster, and you're ready to restore regular operation. Operations are transferred back to original functionality once they're free from the attack.

   This phase of recovery can last weeks or even months, depending on the severity of the attack. Among the activities that can occur in this phase are:
   - continuous monitoring to ensure attack effects are gone,
   - ensuring that all needed infrastructure (power, telecommunications, and security) is functional, and
   - shutting down contingency systems that were activated when the attack began.

   As a reminder, you should periodically execute and test your backup process so that you're fully prepared in situations where reconstitution and restoration are necessary.

Relevant Technical Standards for RC.RP-1

Recovery plan is executed during or after a cybersecurity incident

- CIS CSC 10
- COBIT 5 APO12.06, DSS02.05, DSS03.04
- ISO/IEC 27001:2013 A.16.1.5
- NIST SP 800-53 Rev. 5 CP-10, IR-4, IR-8

B. Update Recovery Procedures Based on New Information as Recovery Gets Underway

(RC.IM-1: Recovery strategies are updated.)

After any incident disaster recovery, conduct thorough and complete documentation of all recovery processes, develop lessons learned and build those lessons into the disaster recovery plan. It's helpful to focus on metrics such as mean time to activation and reconstitution so that you can measure improvement in your disaster response plan in the future.

Relevant Technical Standards for RC.IM-1

Recovery plans incorporate lessons learned

- COBIT 5 BAI01.13
- ISA 62443-2-1:2009 4.3.4.5.10, 4.4.3.4
- ISO/IEC 27001:2013 A.16.1.6, Clause 10
- NIST SP 800-53 Rev. 4 CP-2, IR-4, IR-8

C. Develop Relationships with Media to Accurately Disseminate Information and Engage in Reputational Damage Limitation
(RC.CO-1: Public relations are managed.)

It is crucial to establish good public communications after significant cybersecurity incidents, which must be modulated to be informative but not cause any undue consternation or panic. Invest resources in proactive communications. It is helpful to develop a media plan in advance that can be modified contingent on the attack's nature.

Relevant Technical Standards for RC.CO-1 (and RC.CO-2 Regarding Advance Media Plans)

Public relations are managed

- COBIT 5 EDM03.02
- ISO/IEC 27001:2013 A.6.1.4, Clause 7.4
- COBIT 5 MEA03.02

SUMMARY

Here are some of the central lessons we've learned about developing a continuity of operations plan:

- The first step in developing a response plan is to understand your organization's business needs and develop a plan to assign personnel various responsibilities when responding to an incident.
- Both internal and external communications are the most critical incident response components.
- Make sure to develop communications that work across the organization, including corporate communications, regulatory affairs, legal, compliance and audit, and business operations.

- Analyzing the incident is a crucial component of incident response.
- Any initial report of the incident should include assessing its impacts, such as the ability to access specific systems or sensitive data exposure.
- Preserve evidence, also known as digital forensics, that you can use in pursuing computer crimes.
- Prioritize how you plan to deal with an incident and don't approach it on an ad hoc basis.
- Consider establishing a process for receiving bug reports.
- The first step in risk mitigation is to limit the scope and magnitude of the incident and establish procedures to contain it.
- You can choose to either accept, avoid, or limit incident damage, depending on your strategies and cost trade-offs.
- Recovery from an incident should occur according to three phases: activation, execution, and restitution.
- Update recovery procedures based on new information as recovery gets underway.
- Develop relationships with media in advance to limit reputational damage.

CHAPTER QUIZ

The following short quiz should help you remember some of the disaster recovery concepts introduced in this chapter. Answers can be found at the end of the book.

1. **Which of the following is the most useful first step in establishing a computer security incident response team – your CSIRT? (Select one.)**
   - **a.** Review your IT personnel and select the best and brightest for inclusion on the CSIRT.
   - **b.** Develop an incident response plan and then figure out which personnel are essential to be on the CSIRT.
   - **c.** Scan your organization to select CSIRT members from across the organization, including non-technical personnel.
2. **What is the most critical element in analyzing the cybersecurity incident? (Select one.)**
   - **a.** Prioritizing treatment of the incident.
   - **b.** Gathering and preserving evidence of the incident.
   - **c.** Examining your intrusion detection system.
3. **When it comes to mitigating cybersecurity incidents, which of the following steps will best help stop the incident from spreading through your organization? (Select one.)**
   - **a.** Eliminate the threat and block the adversary.
   - **b.** Take steps to contain the incident.
   - **c.** Analyze the incident in hopes of finding its root causes.
4. **What does an incident recovery plan achieve? (Select all that apply.)**
   - **a.** Helps the organization recoup or recover from any losses that may have occurred during the incident.

b. Helps clarify whether the threat posed by the incident should be accepted, avoided, or limited.

c. Helps the organization come to grips with the damage caused by the incident.

ESSENTIAL READING FOR DEVELOPING A CONTINUITY OF OPERATIONS PLAN

Vladimir Sanchez Padilla and Franklin F. Freire, A Contingency Plan Framework for Cyber-Attacks, *Journal of Information Systems Engineering & Management*, 2019, at https://www.jisem-journal.com/download/a-contingency-plan-framework-for-cyber-attacks-5898.pdf.

Luis Ayala, Cyber-Attack Response and Recovery Planning, *Cybersecurity for Hospitals and Healthcare Facilities*, September 7, 2016, 75–78, at https://link.springer.com/chapter/10.1007/978-1-4842-2155-6_8.

David Sutton, *Business Continuity in a Cyber World: Surviving Cyberattacks* (Business Expert Press, 2018).

Gloria Appiah, Joseph Amankwah-Amoah, and Yu-Lun Liu, Organizational Architecture, Resilience, and Cyberattacks, *IEEE Transactions on Engineering Management*, July 17, 2020, at https://ieeexplore.ieee.org/abstract/document/9143194.

CHAPTER 5

Supply Chain Risk Management

Overview of Chapter and Objective
This chapter will provide the reader with an introduction to the complex and evolving supply chain risk management field. The reader will also learn about the five essential aspects of supply chain risk management in the most recently updated version of the NIST Framework: (1) how to identify where you should manage supply chain risks, (2) pinpointing which suppliers are crucial to supply chain risk management, (3) developing vendor contracts that minimize supply chain risks, (4) continually assessing supply chain risk management procedures, and (5) testing to make sure vendors are resilient in the event of supply disruptions.

Doug's team at Deluxe Security and Surveillance Systems Inc. is developing and installing a new type of motion detection alarm system when the avatar of a junior security engineer, Paige, pops up in a group chat on the company's secure comms channel. "That's odd," Doug thinks. He just saw Paige leave the building's tightly controlled facility, saying something about a dental appointment. He steps out of his office and sticks his head into Paige's office near the server room. She's not there.

"She must be somewhere else in the building," Doug says to himself – this particular comms channel is accessible only from Deluxe's secure location. He continues working. Paige's avatar stays in the group chat. After a few hours, he sees Paige walk by his office door. He glances up from his mobile phone to look at his desktop screen and sees not one but two of Paige's avatars. Something's

Cybersecurity Risk Management: Mastering the Fundamentals Using the NIST Cybersecurity Framework, First Edition. Cynthia Brumfield and Brian Haugli.

not right. He goes into Paige's office and can instantly tell she's intent on figuring out how two of her avatars are on the screen.

After an emergency team meeting to get to the bottom of the mystery, one lead security engineer discovers the problem. An unknown actor has duplicated Paige's account and is pinging a server overseas from that account. But how did the intruder gain access?

Following days of digging by every technical staff member at the company, the answer becomes clear. Someone, a sophisticated actor, embedded spyware in an update to the video monitoring system software used by the company in its cameras, which has been installed in two dozen naval bases across the world.

More round-the-clock, days-long investigations by the all-hands team reveal that thousands of facilities that deploy the same cameras across the federal government and corporate campuses have also been affected by the same spyware. Deluxe Security might not have caught this massive supply chain breach but for the double avatars that appeared after Paige returned from her dental appointment.

INTRODUCTION

As the situation involving Deluxe's infected software update illustrates, a breach in any organization's supply chain can spell significant trouble, and supply chain infections can encompass a massive number of users. The information and operational technologies that organizations use daily rely on a complex, interconnected, multinational supply chain of hardware, software, and services stemming from diverse sources and multiple layers of manufacturers, distributors, contractors, and subcontractors. This vast supply chain consists of public- and private-sector organizations worldwide that design, manufacture, distribute, and deploy technology solutions, products, and services.

These components combine to increase the complexity, diversity, and scale of the threats introduced into any organization's operations at any point in the supply chain ecosystem. These threats can include insertion of counterfeits, unauthorized production, tampering, theft, insertion of malicious software and hardware, as well as poor manufacturing and development practices.

Managing all of these supply chain risks is a complex, time-consuming, and detailed challenge, made all the more so by the sophistication of often well-resourced malicious actors, such as nation-state threat groups. Managing these risks also requires a multifaceted, coordinated effort that builds trust relationships with internal and external stakeholders.

For all these reasons, managing supply chain risks is a still-evolving, wide-ranging, technically complex topic that can take years and intensive study to understand. In this section, you'll read about some critical supply chain risk management developments, and we'll walk you through some of the high-level concepts you should know as you approach this critical topic.

I. NIST SPECIAL PUBLICATION 800-161

Before we discuss the supply chain provisions in the NIST Framework, it's helpful to flag an essential NIST resource that many in the cybersecurity arena consider the definitive document in managing supply chain risks. In

2015, NIST released *Supply Chain Risk Management Practices for Federal Information Systems and Organizations*. This detailed document spells out the supply chain risk management practices that federal systems administrators should follow. Referred to as 800-161, it is considered by many information security professionals to be the touchstone for supply chain risk management.

Currently under revision, 800-161 is designed to help federal agencies in "identifying, assessing, selecting, and implementing risk management processes and mitigating controls throughout their organizations to help manage" supply chain risks. Although it contains no guidance for entities outside the federal government, many high-profile organizations rely on this in-depth resource as a reference for good supply chain security practices.

II. SOFTWARE BILL OF MATERIALS

A software bill of materials (SBOM) is simply a list of the individual components that make up any given piece of software, given almost all software developers' virtually universal use of third-party features.

This list of ingredients allows for more rapid identification of potential software vulnerabilities and supports better software purchasing decisions, among other benefits. According to the National Telecommunications and Information Administration (NTIA), an arm of the Department of Commerce, an SBOM is "a formal record containing the details and supply chain relationships of various components used in building software An SBOM is effectively a nested inventory: a list of ingredients that make up software components."

Voices of Experience
On Supply Chain

Enterprises Need a Consistent Approach

Enterprises need to develop a consistent approach to evaluating those suppliers and it starts with determining what their appetite for risk is and what are the key business outcomes that are tied to that supplier.

We've seen with COVID-19 that there are often far more interdependencies than people realize in getting that product to market safely and securely. So, you ask questions like: Does your vendor have a single source supply chain? Are they applying best practices end-to-end? That means sourcing, development, testing, deployment, integration, operations, maintenance, and on-and-on.

What will determine the security of the network you are trying to build is the security of the products and the deployments, the configurations, and the operational procedures that are put on top of all the standardized functions and capabilities that you are checking the boxes on.

Jason Boswell, Head of Security, Network Product Solutions, Ericsson, North America

In 2018, the NTIA established a cross-sector, industry-led, multi-stake-holder process on Software Component Transparency to better understand the potential, benefits, and possible drawbacks to better software transparency through an SBOM. This non-regulatory effort has looked at the security and economic benefits of SBOMs and identified existing standards that developers can use to convey SBOM data automatically. The NTIA maintains a dedicated page (https://www.ntia.gov/SBOM) filled with fact sheets and resources surrounding the SBOM.

III. NIST REVISED FRAMEWORK INCORPORATES MAJOR SUPPLY CHAIN CATEGORY

NIST's updated Cybersecurity Framework, released in April 2018, incorporated a new category, Supply Chain (SC), under the Identify function, and five new subcategories that deal with desired outcomes for supply chain risk management. This new guidance provides organizations with broad steps to help you gain greater visibility into how you can incorporate supply chain management into your organization's overall risk assessment strategy.

The following sections briefly highlight the new subcategories of the Framework that deal with supply chain issues.

A. Identify, Establish, and Assess Cyber Supply Chain Risk Management Processes and Gain Stakeholder Agreement

(ID.SC-1: Cyber supply chain risk management processes are identified, established, assessed, managed, and agreed to by organizational stakeholders.)

The first step in supply chain risk management is determining where you need to manage those risks within your organization by assessing where the likely failure points might occur due to supply chain risks. This identification process is often coupled with the concept of supply chain resilience, meaning identifying those points in your technology configuration that could cause operational failure due to lack of robustness.

Key areas to identify are vendor access points into your organization or product development pipeline, subcontractors used by vendors, software packages being deployed, and maintenance windows. Determine whether any vendors or contractors have access to intellectual property, customer data, or infrastructure.

After this identification, you should consider establishing processes for managing these supply chain risks and assessing their workability and day-to-day management requirements. Once satisfied with the procedures established, gaining agreement among organizational stakeholders, including non-technical personnel across the organization, such as accounting departments, legal departments, and more, is crucial for any supply chain risk management process.

Relevant Technical Standards for ID.SC-1

Cyber supply chain risk management processes are identified, established, assessed, managed, and agreed to by organizational stakeholders

- CIS CSC 4
- COBIT 5 APO10.01, APO10.04, APO12.04, APO12.05, APO13.02, BAI01.03, BAI02.03, BAI04.02
- ISA 62443-2-1:2009 4.3.4.2
- ISO/IEC 27001:2013 A.15.1.1, A.15.1.2, A.15.1.3, A.15.2.1, A.15.2.2
- NIST SP 800-53 Rev. 4 SA-9, SA-12, PM-9

B. Identify, Prioritize, and Assess Suppliers and Third-Party Partners of Suppliers

(ID.SC-2: Suppliers and third-party partners of information systems, components, and services are identified, prioritized, and assessed using a cyber supply chain risk assessment process.)

As is the case for the overall organization's risk management practices, identifying suppliers is critical to supply chain risk management. In the context of the supply chain, however, it's essential also to know and identify the partners of your organization's suppliers to better enable tracking of supply chain risks.

After identifying suppliers and their partners, prioritize them according to the supply chain risk assessment processes you've established to better target resources in tracking and mitigating risks. This prioritization should include who the vendors are and the services they are providing.

You should then prioritize those services to your organization based on importance to revenue lines, business functions, service delivery, customer access, software deployment capabilities, or other factors determined by leadership and management.

A basic rubric to assess suppliers and vendors could start with the vendors' access and importance to the organization. Think of these on an X- and Y-axis. Those with a high value to the business and a high level of access would be in the upper right. You should scrutinize these vendors the most. Conversely, those with a low level of value and a low level of access may not require as much of an in-depth assessment.

Relevant Technical Standards for ID.SC-2

Suppliers and third-party partners of information systems, components, and services are identified, prioritized, and assessed using a cyber supply chain risk assessment process

- COBIT 5 APO10.01, APO10.02, APO10.04, APO10.05, APO12.01, APO12.02, APO12.03, APO12.04, APO12.05, APO12.06, APO13.02, BAI02.03
- ISA 62443-2-1:2009 4.2.3.1, 4.2.3.2, 4.2.3.3, 4.2.3.4, 4.2.3.6, 4.2.3.8, 4.2.3.9, 4.2.3.10, 4.2.3.12, 4.2.3.13, 4.2.3.14
- ISO/IEC 27001:2013 A.15.2.1, A.15.2.2
- NIST SP 800-53 Rev. 4 RA-2, RA-3, SA-12, SA-14, SA-15, PM-9

C. Develop Contracts with Suppliers and Third-Party Partners to Address Your Organization's Supply Chain Risk Management Goals

(ID.SC-3: Contracts with suppliers and third-party partners are used to implement appropriate measures designed to meet the objectives of an organization's cybersecurity program and Cyber Supply Chain Risk Management Plan.)

Because supply chain risk management deals by definition with your organization's suppliers and third-party partners, it's essential to communicate your organization's needs to those suppliers and third-party partners consistent with your own risk assessment plan. The time to start sharing with your suppliers and third-party partners is during the contracting process.

The following are some key points to raise during the contracting process with your suppliers and partners so that you can incorporate the necessary provisions in your contracts.

- Ensure your vendors understand how critical cybersecurity is to your organization and offer as many specific details about your cybersecurity needs as possible.
- Ask them to provide documentation and proof of their commitments to establishing and maintaining security. This documentation could include attestations to written policies, the contact information of a named cybersecurity leader or CISO, penetration test results, or third-party certified audits conducted within the past 6–12 months.
- Stress to them the importance of knowing how they ensure that *their* vendors are abiding by the necessary security protocols and ask them to provide documentation and proof of how they monitor their vendors' security.
- Ensure that your suppliers and vendors have operating procedures and recovery plans to carry out during service disruptions and ask them to spell out how often they will jointly practice business resumption and disaster recovery plans.
- Do not rely on one-time statements or documentation from your vendors or contractors but instead continuously monitor them to detect changes in their networks and ask them to remediate any issues that emerge immediately.
- The most impactful team to assemble draws from the legal, IT, procurement, and cybersecurity groups. Having these teams empower the procurement group to understand cybersecurity and its risks better will allow for a more efficient contract process. If not, a back-and-forth between procurement and the cybersecurity group could create bottlenecks and delays in onboarding vendors or suppliers to support critical business initiatives.

Relevant Technical Standards for ID.SC-3

Contracts with suppliers and third-party partners are used to implement appropriate measures designed to meet the objectives of an organization's cybersecurity program and Cyber Supply Chain Risk Management Plan

- COBIT 5 APO10.01, APO10.02, APO10.03, APO10.04, APO10.05
- ISA 62443-2-1:2009 4.3.2.6.4, 4.3.2.6.7
- ISO/IEC 27001:2013 A.15.1.1, A.15.1.2, A.15.1.3
- NIST SP 800-53 Rev. 4 SA-9, SA-11, SA-12, PM-9

D. Routinely Assess Suppliers and Third-Party Partners Using Audits, Test Results, and Other Forms of Evaluation

(ID.SC-4: Suppliers and third-party partners are routinely assessed using audits, test results, or other forms of evaluations to confirm they are meeting their contractual obligations.)

It's essential to build into your supplier and consultant contracts provisions that address your cybersecurity needs. It's equally important to establish formal programs such as audits, test results, and other forms of evaluations to ensure they are meeting their contractual obligations for supply chain security. These evaluations should be included as part of your standard cybersecurity governance processes and structure. For very vital suppliers or vendors, you should know their cyber leadership and involve them in your risk management.

Some factors to consider in conducting such an audit or evaluation according to a NIST case study as part of its Best Practices in Cyber Supply Chain Risk Management prepared by Boeing and Exostar (https://www.nist.gov/system/files/documents/itl/csd/NIST_USRP-Boeing-Exostar-Case-Study.pdf) are:

- Control and monitor user and administrative accounts from accessing the applications, systems, or networks.
- Check to see that you give only authorized devices access and prevent unauthorized or unmanaged devices from gaining access.
- Check to see that only authorized software is installed and can execute and that unauthorized and unmanaged software is found and prevented from installation or execution.
- Establish, implement, and actively manage the security configuration of laptops, servers, and workstations using a rigorous configuration management and change control process.
- Ensure that controls are in place to prevent attackers from exploiting vulnerable services and settings.
- Acquire, assess, and take action on new information to identify and remediate vulnerabilities and minimize the window of opportunity for attackers.

This case study is based primarily on the Center for Internet Security (CIS) Critical Security Controls. The alignment of NIST CSF Controls and the CIS Critical Security Controls can be found in Appendix B.

Relevant Technical Standards for ID.SC-4

Suppliers and third-party partners are routinely assessed using audits, test results, or other forms of evaluations to confirm they are meeting their contractual obligations

- COBIT 5 APO10.01, APO10.03, APO10.04, APO10.05, MEA01.01, MEA01.02, MEA01.03, MEA01.04, MEA01.05
- ISA 62443-2-1:2009 4.3.2.6.7
- ISA 62443-3-3:2013 SR 6.1
- ISO/IEC 27001:2013 A.15.2.1, A.15.2.2
- NIST SP 800-53 Rev. 4 AU-2, AU-6, AU-12, AU-16, PS-7, SA-9, SA-12

E.   Test to Make Sure Your Suppliers and Third-Party Providers Can Respond to and Recover from Service Disruption

(ID.SC-5: Response and recovery planning and testing are conducted with suppliers and third-party providers.)

Just as your organization should have its own disaster and recovery plans, your suppliers and other third-party providers should have their own disaster and recovery plans in place to deal with service disruptions due to a cyber incident or other causes. An essential part of supply chain security is working with your suppliers, particularly your high-risk vendors, to plan for recovery together and periodically test those plans.

Among just *some* of the many elements of disaster recovery that you should consider asking your suppliers and other third parties to embrace are:

- establishing a specified time frame for resuming activities and recovering data after a service disruption,
- implementing a telecommunications redundancy and resilience plan,
- preparing for known and emerging threats and vulnerabilities,
- examining physical and environmental controls to ensure the safety and security of facilities, and
- devising an incident reporting and management program to ensure you have clearly documented processes and accountability checks.

Relevant Technical Standards for ID.SC-5

Response and recovery planning and testing are conducted with suppliers and third-party providers

- COBIT 5 APO10.01, APO10.03, APO10.04, APO10.05, MEA01.01, MEA01.02, MEA01.03, MEA01.04, MEA01.05
- ISA 62443-2-1:2009 4.3.2.6.7

> - ISA 62443-3-3:2013 SR 6.1
> - ISO/IEC 27001:2013 A.15.2.1, A.15.2.2
> - NIST SP 800-53 Rev. 4 AU-2, AU-6, AU-12, AU-16, PS-7, SA-9, SA-12

SUMMARY

Here are some of the main takeaways on supply chain security from this chapter:

- The first steps you should take in managing supply chain risks are identifying where the likely failure points might occur due to supply chain risks and then prioritizing them.
- You should establish supply chain risk management processes and assess their workability and day-to-day management requirements based on feedback and buy-in from organizational technical and non-technical stakeholders.
- Identifying your suppliers is critical to supply chain risk management, as is identifying the partners of your organization's suppliers to enable tracking of supply chain risks better.
- Prioritize your suppliers and their partners according to your supply chain risk management processes.
- Communicate your organization's needs to those suppliers and third-party partners consistent with your own risk assessment plan and ensure you adequately consider them in the contracting process.
- Establish formal programs such as audits, test results, and other forms of evaluations to ensure contractors are meeting their contractual obligations for supply chain security.
- Ask your suppliers about their disaster recovery plans and work with them, particularly your high-risk vendors, to plan for recovery together and to test those plans periodically.

CHAPTER QUIZ

The following short quiz should help you better remember some of the critical supply chain risk management concepts introduced in this chapter. Answers can be found at the end of the book.

1. **What should be your first step in managing supply chain risks? (Select one.)**
   a. Establish processes for managing supply chain risks and assess their workability.
   b. Communicate your organization's cybersecurity needs to your suppliers and their suppliers.
   c. Determine where you need to manage those risks within your organization by assessing where the likely failure points might occur due to supply chain risks.

		Maintain Human Safety	Maintain Environmental Safety	Maintain Quality of Product	Maintain Production Goals	Maintain Trade Secrets
	Category	Subcategories				
ID	Asset Management	ID.AM-1	ID.AM-1	ID.AM-1	ID.AM-1	ID.AM-1
		ID.AM-2	ID.AM-2	ID.AM-2	ID.AM-2	ID.AM-2
		ID.AM-3	ID.AM-3	ID.AM-3	ID.AM-3	ID.AM-3
		ID.AM-4	ID.AM-4	ID.AM-4	ID.AM-4	ID.AM-4
		ID.AM-5	ID.AM-5	ID.AM-5	ID.AM-5	ID.AM-5
		ID.AM-6	ID.AM-6	ID.AM-6	ID.AM-6	ID.AM-6
	Business Environment	ID.BE-1	ID.BE-1	ID.BE-1	ID.BE-1	ID.BE-1
		ID.BE-2	ID.BE-2	ID.BE-2	ID.BE-2	ID.BE-2
		ID.BE-3	ID.BE-3	ID.BE-3	ID.BE-3	ID.BE-3
		ID.BE-4	ID.BE-4	ID.BE-4	ID.BE-4	ID.BE-4
		ID.BE-5	ID.BE-5	ID.BE-5	ID.BE-5	ID.BE-5
	Governance	ID.GV-1	ID.GV-1	ID.GV-1	ID.GV-1	ID.GV-1
		ID.GV-2	ID.GV-2	ID.GV-2	ID.GV-2	ID.GV-2
		ID.GV-3	ID.GV-3	ID.GV-3	ID.GV-3	ID.GV-3
		ID.GV-4	ID.GV-4	ID.GV-4	ID.GV-4	ID.GV-4
	Risk Assessment	ID.RA-1	ID.RA-1	ID.RA-1	ID.RA-1	ID.RA-1
		ID.RA-2	ID.RA-2	ID.RA-2	ID.RA-2	ID.RA-2
		ID.RA-3	ID.RA-3	ID.RA-3	ID.RA-3	ID.RA-3
		ID.RA-4	ID.RA-4	ID.RA-4	ID.RA-4	ID.RA-4
		ID.RA-5	ID.RA-5	ID.RA-5	ID.RA-5	ID.RA-5
		ID.RA-6	ID.RA-6	ID.RA-6	ID.RA-6	ID.RA-6
	Risk Management Strategy	ID.RM-1	ID.RM-1	ID.RM-1	ID.RM-1	ID.RM-1
		ID.RM-2	ID.RM-2	ID.RM-2	ID.RM-2	ID.RM-2
		ID.RM-3	ID.RM-3	ID.RM-3	ID.RM-3	ID.RM-3
	Supply Chain Management	ID.SC-1	ID.SC-1	ID.SC-1	ID.SC-1	ID.SC-1
		ID.SC-2	ID.SC-2	ID.SC-2	ID.SC-2	ID.SC-2
		ID.SC-3	ID.SC-3	ID.SC-3	ID.SC-3	ID.SC-3
		ID.SC-4	ID.SC-4	ID.SC-4	ID.SC-4	ID.SC-4
		ID.SC-5	ID.SC-5	ID.SC-5	ID.SC-5	ID.SC-5

FIGURE 6.1 Function and Category Unique Identifiers.

Respond (Figure 6.4), and Recover (Figure 6.5) – the "Manufacturing Profile" is intended to provide manufacturers with:

- a method to identify opportunities for improving the current cybersecurity posture of the manufacturing system,
- an evaluation of their ability to operate the control environment at their acceptable risk level, and
- a standardized approach to preparing the cybersecurity plan for ongoing assurance of the manufacturing system's security.

As is true of the categories and subcategories of the Framework itself, the Manufacturing "Target" Profile focuses on desired cybersecurity outcomes to reveal gaps between where an organization's cybersecurity profile stands currently and where it ideally should be. And, as is true with the regular Framework, one key goal of the Manufacturing Profile is to provide a means to communicate the organization's security status to outside stakeholders, including suppliers, service providers, investors, auditors, and, in some circumstances, regulators and policy-makers.

	Category	Maintain Human Safety	Maintain Environmental Safety	Maintain Quality of Product	Maintain Production Goals	Maintain Trade Secrets
	Category	Subcategories				
RC	Recovery Planning	RC.RP-1	RC.RP-1	RC.RP-1	RC.RP-1	RC.RP-1
	Improvements	RC.IM-1	RC.IM-1	RC.IM-1	RC.IM-1	RC.IM-1
		RC.IM-2	RC.IM-2	RC.IM-2	RC.IM-2	RC.IM-2
	Communications	RC.CO-1	RC.CO-1	RC.CO-1	RC.CO-1	RC.CO-1
		RC.CO-2	RC.CO-2	RC.CO-2	RC.CO-2	RC.CO-2
		RC.CO-3	RC.CO-3	RC.CO-3	RC.CO-3	RC.CO-3

FIGURE 6.5 Function and Category Unique Recovery Elements.

Unlike the main Framework, the Manufacturing Profile focuses heavily on operational technology used to run machines and equipment and manufacturing processes. NIST has oriented the Profile to speak to a wide range of technically adept audiences, from control engineers, integrators, and architects who design or implement secure manufacturing systems to academics researching the unique security aspects of manufacturing.

The Manufacturing Profile focuses on industrial control systems (ICS), including supervisory control and data acquisition (SCADA) systems, distributed control systems (DCSs), and other control system configurations such as programmable logic controllers (PLCs) often found in the industrial sectors and critical infrastructures. This broad-based profile can be distinguished from security frameworks and profiles that focus on particular industrial sectors such as those that make up the power grid environment.

According to NIST, industrial control systems fall into one of two categories: process-based, which encompasses continuous or batch manufacturing, or discrete-based, which is a series of operations to create a specific end product, or a combination of both. The industrial control roadmap includes identifying five common business/mission objectives of the manufacturing sector. These objectives are to Maintain Human Safety, Maintain Environmental Safety, Maintain Quality of Product, Maintain Production Goals, and Maintain Trade Secrets.

The Profile subcategories are prioritized to support specific business/mission objectives, enabling organizations to implement "measures against threats that could directly and severely compromise their ability to perform their essential mission." For each mission objective, NIST has developed matrices for the significant function categories and highlighted the most critical subcategories, which may not apply to all manufacturers.

In its guidance, NIST provides *low*, *moderate*, and *high* impact level configurations that organizations can use to "identify the security capability, functionality, and specificity for supporting manufacturing systems based on the categorization of the manufacturing system." Speaking generally, low is defined by NIST as a potential impact that could have a *limited* effect on operations, product, assets, image, finances, personnel, the general public, or the environment. A moderate impact could have a *serious* effect on all of the same aspects as low impact level configurations, while high impact has *severe or catastrophic* adverse effects.

ESSENTIAL READING ON MANUFACTURING AND INDUSTRIAL CONTROL SECURITY

Dragos, Inc., *Combating Cyber Attacks with Consequence-Driven ICS Cybersecurity*, https://www.dragos.com/blog/industry-news/combating-cyber-attacks-with-consequence-driven-ics-cybersecurity.

Andrew A. Bochman and Sarah Freeman, *Countering Cyber Sabotage: Introducing Consequence-Driven, Cyber-Informed Engineering* (CCE, 1st ed.) at https://www.amazon.com/Countering-Cyber-Sabotage-Consequence-Driven-Cyber-Informed/dp/036749115X.

Helge Janicke, Kevin Jones, and Thomas Brandstetter (eds), *4th International Symposium for ICS & SCADA Cyber Security Research 2016* at https://www.amazon.com/dp/1780173571?tag=uuid10-20.

Appendix A: Helpful Advice for Small Organizations Seeking to Implement Some of the Book's Recommendations

Many, if not most, of the principles and practices of sound cybersecurity presented throughout this book are admittedly complex. They are also far easier to grasp and implement for large organizations, which typically have bigger budgets and multiple personnel to devote to IT, technology, security tasks, and training.

Numerous resources offer guidance to small and medium-sized businesses when implementing the NIST Cybersecurity Framework and adopting critical practices to protecting systems and information. Three in particular that are worth reviewing and keeping on hand are:

1. NISTIR 7621, Revision 1 – *Small Business Information Security: The Fundamentals*, November 2016 at https://nvlpubs.nist.gov/nistpubs/ir/2016/NIST.IR.7621r1.pdf.
2. NIST Small Business Cybersecurity Corner at https://www.nist.gov/itl/smallbusinesscyber.
3. Cybersecurity Risk Management and Best Practices (CSRIC IV WG4 Final Report), Section 9.9 Small and Medium Business (370–397) at https://transition.fcc.gov/pshs/advisory/csric4/CSRIC_IV_WG4_Final_Report_031815.pdf.

However, even these guides detail, albeit more simply, the same basic cybersecurity steps that are highlighted in this book – developing risk assessments, mapping out and planning infrastructure protections, implementing intrusion detection systems, and so forth.

What this means, in short, is that there is no easy way to ensure systems and assets remain safe other than completing the complex, often tedious,

Cybersecurity Risk Management: Mastering the Fundamentals Using the NIST Cybersecurity Framework, First Edition. Cynthia Brumfield and Brian Haugli.
© 2022 Cynthia Brumfield and Brian Haugli. Published 2022 by John Wiley & Sons, Inc.

and usually laborious, repetitive, and ongoing steps that are designed to provide protective layers and recovery processes for your organization.

With this caveat in mind, there are a few steps you can take as a small organization to move closer to the full range of cybersecurity practices needed as the complexity of protecting digital assets grows. Here are a few recommendations:

1. **Trusted Personnel Should Wear Multiple Hats:** If your organization consists of only a small number of personnel, adapt some of the strategies listed below and in the other chapters so that a handful of trusted personnel can carry them out. You can assign the roles and responsibilities that are usually delegated across personnel in larger organizations to however many personnel you trust. For example, in devising an incident response team, which in a larger organization might rely on human resources, legal, public relations, and IT personnel, brainstorm how the discrete responsibilities of all those functions might be handled by a systems administrator and an office manager, for example.

2. **Focus on the Basics First:** Perform a risk assessment to determine what controls and capabilities you have in place. Once gaps are identified, start remediating deficiencies. This assessment should cover basic cyber hygiene such as multi-factor authentication, separate administrative credentials, e-mail security, scheduled patching programs, firewall/perimeter controls, and host-based detection and response software. These foundational controls address the highest likelihood vulnerabilities that small organizations will have.

3. **Bring in Outside Help:** When budgeting for IT and technical resources, advocate for funds that you can use to bring in outside help when needed. External cybersecurity consultants can help your organization figure out how to make changes that improve your security posture or assist in a crisis when all employees are overtaxed. Good cybersecurity consultants can help you establish practices ahead of time that can save you grief when an incident does occur and can also help you select your cybersecurity configuration so that the impact of security incidents can be lessened. Fees for external consultants can range from modest amounts to significant financial outlays if you wait to hire the consultants during a crisis.

4. **Gather Evidence and Materials to Advocate for More Security Resources:** Make it a habit of staying on top of the adverse cybersecurity experiences of other organizations so that you can develop a cybersecurity resource "arsenal" to fight for more resources, whether personnel resources or funds for outside consultants. Network with your peers to find out what they're doing to gather your evidence to advocate for more security resources.

Appendix B: Critical Security Controls Version 8.0 Mapped to NIST CSF v1.1

There are several control frameworks available to address the more tactical elements of cybersecurity. One industry-recognized framework is the Center for Internet Security (CIS) Controls, formerly known as the SANS Top 20. This mapping demonstrates connections between NIST Cybersecurity Framework (CSF) and the CIS Controls Version 8.0. The CIS Controls provide security best practices to help organizations defend assets in cyberspace.

Use this mapping to help identify specific technical implementations, modifications, or best practices that can aid in meeting a respective NIST CSF Subcategory Control. (Please note that not all CIS elements map directly to the NIST Framework.)

CIS Sub-Control	CIS Control	NIST CSF
	Inventory and Control of Hardware Assets	
1.1	Establish and Maintain Detailed Asset Inventory	ID.AM-1
		PR.DS-3
1.2	Address Unauthorized Assets	
1.3	Utilize an Active Discovery Tool	DE.CM-7
1.4	Use Dynamic Host Configuration Protocol (DHCP) Logging to Update Enterprise Asset Inventory	DE.CM-7
1.5	Use a Passive Asset Discovery Tool	DE.CM-7
	Inventory and Control of Software Assets	
2.1	Establish and Maintain a Software Inventory	ID.AM-2
2.2	Ensure Authorized Software is Currently Supported	ID.AM-2
2.3	Address Unauthorized Software	DE.CM-7

(Continued)

Cybersecurity Risk Management: Mastering the Fundamentals Using the NIST Cybersecurity Framework, First Edition. Cynthia Brumfield and Brian Haugli.
© 2022 Cynthia Brumfield and Brian Haugli. Published 2022 by John Wiley & Sons, Inc.

(Continued)

CIS Sub-Control	CIS Control	NIST CSF
2.4	Utilize Automated Software Inventory Tools	DE.CM-7
2.5	Allowlist Authorized Software	DE.CM-7
2.6	Allowlist Authorized Libraries	DE.CM-7
2.7	Allowlist Authorized Scripts	PR.IP-1
		PR.PT-3
	Data Protection	
3.1	Establish and Maintain a Data Management Process	PR.IP-6
3.2	Establish and Maintain a Data Inventory	ID.AM-5
3.3	Configure Data Access Control Lists	PR.AC-4
3.4	Enforce Data Retention	
3.5	Securely Dispose of Data	PR.DS-3
		PR.IP-6
3.6	Encrypt Data on End-User Devices	
3.7	Establish and Maintain a Data Classification Scheme	ID.AM-5
		ID.RA-5
3.8	Document Data Flows	DE.AE-1
		ID.AM-3
3.9	Encrypt Data on Removable Media	PR.PT-2
3.10	Encrypt Sensitive Data in Transit	PR.DS-2
3.11	Encrypt Sensitive Data at Rest	PR.DS-1
3.12	Segment Data Processing and Storage Based on Sensitivity	PR.AC-5
3.13	Deploy a Data Loss Prevention Solution	PR.DS-5
3.14	Log Sensitive Data Access	
	Secure Configuration of Enterprise Assets and Software	
4.1	Establish and Maintain a Secure Configuration Process	PR.IP-1
4.2	Establish and Maintain a Secure Configuration Process for Network Infrastructure	PR.IP-1
4.3	Configure Automatic Session Locking on Enterprise Assets	PR.IP-1
4.4	Implement and Manage a Firewall on Servers	
4.5	Implement and Manage a Firewall on End-User Devices	
4.6	Securely Manage Enterprise Assets and Software	
4.7	Manage Default Accounts on Enterprise Assets and Software	PR.AC-1
4.8	Uninstall or Disable Unnecessary Services on Enterprise Assets and Software	
4.9	Configure Trusted DNS Servers on Enterprise Assets	
4.10	Enforce Automatic Device Lockout on Portable End-User Devices	
4.11	Enforce Remote Wipe Capability on Portable End-User Devices	PR.AC-3
4.12	Separate Enterprise Workspaces on Mobile End-User Devices	

(Continued)

CIS Sub-Control	CIS Control	NIST CSF
	Account Management	
5.1	Establish and Maintain an Inventory of Accounts	PR.AC-1
5.2	Use Unique Passwords	
5.3	Disable Dormant Accounts	PR.AC-1
5.4	Restrict Administrator Privileges to Dedicated Administrator Accounts	PR.AC-4
5.5	Establish and Maintain an Inventory of Service Accounts	PR.AC-1
5.6	Centralize Account Management	
	Access Control Management	
6.1	Establish an Access Granting Process	PR.AC-1
6.2	Establish an Access Revoking Process	PR.AC-1 PR.IP-11
6.3	Require MFA for Externally Exposed Applications	PR.AC-7
6.4	Require MFA for Remote Network Access	PR.AC-7 PR.AC-3
6.5	Require MFA for Administrative Access	PR.AC-7
6.6	Establish and Maintain an Inventory of Authentication and Authorization Systems	PR.AC-1 PR.AC-3
6.7	Centralize Access Control	PR.AC-1
6.8	Define and Maintain Role-Based Access Control	PR.AC-4
	Continuous Vulnerability Management	
7.1	Establish and Maintain a Vulnerability Management Process	ID.RA-1
7.2	Establish and Maintain a Remediation Process	ID.RA-1
7.3	Perform Automated Operating System Patch Management	
7.4	Perform Automated Application Patch Management	ID.RA-1
7.5	Perform Automated Vulnerability Scans of Internal Enterprise Assets	DE.CM-8
7.6	Perform Automated Vulnerability Scans of Externally Exposed Enterprise Assets	ID.RA-5 PR.IP-12
7.7	Remediate Detected Vulnerabilities	
	Audit Log Management	
8.1	Establish and Maintain an Audit Log Management Process	
8.2	Collect Audit Logs	PR.PT-1 DE.AE-3
8.3	Ensure Adequate Audit Log Storage	
8.4	Standardize Time Synchronization	PR.PT-1
8.5	Collect Detailed Audit Logs	DE.AE-3 DE.CM-1

(Continued)

(Continued)

CIS Sub-Control	CIS Control	NIST CSF
8.6	Collect DNS Query Audit Logs	DE.AE-3
8.7	Collect URL Request Audit Logs	DE.AE-3
8.8	Collect Command-Line Audit Logs	PR.PT-1
		DE.AE-3
8.9	Centralize Audit Logs	
8.10	Retain Audit Logs	
8.11	Conduct Audit Log Reviews	PR.PT-1
		RS.AN-1
		DE.AE-2
8.12	Collect Service Provider Logs	DE.AE-3
	Email and Web Browser Protections	
9.1	Ensure Use of Only Fully Supported Browsers and Email Clients	PR.IP-1
9.2	Use DNS Filtering Services	PR.AC-5
9.3	Maintain and Enforce Network-Based URL Filters	PR.AC-5
9.4	Restrict Unnecessary or Unauthorized Browser and Email Client Extensions	PR.IP-1
9.5	Implement DMARC	
9.6	Block Unnecessary File Types	DE.CM-7
		PR.AC-5
9.7	Deploy and Maintain Email Server Anti-Malware Protections	DE.CM-4
	Malware Defenses	
10.1	Deploy and Maintain Anti-Malware Software	DE.CM-4
10.2	Configure Automatic Anti-Malware Signature Updates	DE.CM-4
10.3	Disable Autorun and Autoplay for Removable Media	PR.PT-2
10.4	Configure Automatic Anti-Malware Scanning of Removable Media	DE.CM-4
10.5	Enable Anti-Exploitation Features	DE.CM-4
10.6	Centrally Manage Anti-Malware Software	DE.CM-4
10.7	Use Behavior-Based Anti-Malware Software	DE.CM-4
	Data Recovery	
11.1	Establish and Maintain a Data Recovery Process	PR.IP-9
		ID.SC-5
11.2	Perform Automated Backups	PR.IP-4
11.3	Protect Recovery Data	PR.IP-4
11.4	Establish and Maintain an Isolated Instance of Recovery Data	PR.PT-5
11.5	Test Data Recovery	PR.DS-6
	Network Infrastructure Management	
12.1	Ensure Network Infrastructure is Up-to-Date	
12.2	Establish and Maintain a Secure Network Architecture	PR.AC-5
12.3	Securely Manage Network Infrastructure	PR.AC-7
		PR.DS-2

(Continued)

CIS Sub-Control	CIS Control	NIST CSF
12.4	Establish and Maintain Architecture Diagram(s)	ID.AM-4
12.5	Centralize Network Authentication, Authorization, and Auditing (AAA)	
12.6	Use of Secure Network Management and Communication Protocols	PR.AC-7 PR.DS-2
12.7	Ensure Remote Devices Utilize a VPN and are Connecting to an Enterprise's AAA Infrastructure	PR.AC-3 PR.AC-7
12.8	Establish and Maintain Dedicated Computing Resources for All Administrative Work	PR.AC-5
	Network Monitoring and Defense	
13.1	Centralize Security Event Alerting	
13.2	Deploy a Host-Based Intrusion Detection Solution	DE.CM-1
13.3	Deploy a Network Intrusion Detection Solution	DE.CM-1
13.4	Perform Traffic Filtering Between Network Segments	PR.AC-5
13.5	Manage Access Control for Remote Assets	PR.AC-3 PR.AC-7 PR.MA-2 DE.CM-7
13.6	Collect Network Traffic Flow Logs	DE.CM-1
13.7	Deploy a Host-Based Intrusion Prevention Solution	DE.CM-1
13.8	Deploy a Network Intrusion Prevention Solution	DE.CM-1
13.9	Deploy Port-Level Access Control	PR.AC-1
13.10	Perform Application Layer Filtering	PR.PT-3
13.11	Tune Security Event Alerting Thresholds	DE.AE-5
	Security Awareness and Skills Training	
14.1	Establish and Maintain a Security Awareness Program	ID.AM-6
14.1	Establish and Maintain a Security Awareness Program	ID.GV-1 PR.AT-1
14.2	Train Workforce Members to Recognize Social Engineering Attacks	PR.AT-1
14.3	Train Workforce Members on Authentication Best Practices	PR.AT-1
14.4	Train Workforce on Data Handling Best Practices	PR.AT-1
14.5	Train Workforce Members on Causes of Unintentional Data Exposure	PR.AT-1
14.6	Train Workforce Members on Recognizing and Reporting Security Incidents	PR.AT-1
14.7	Train Workforce on How to Identify and Report if Their Enterprise Assets are Missing Security Updates	PR.AT-1

(Continued)

(Continued)

CIS Sub-Control	CIS Control	NIST CSF
14.8	Train Workforce on the Dangers of Connecting to and Transmitting Enterprise Data Over Insecure Networks	PR.AT-1
14.9	Conduct Role-Specific Security Awareness and Skills Training	PR.AT-1 PR.AT-2 PR.AT-4 PR.AT-5
	Service Provider Management	
15.1	Establish and Maintain an Inventory of Service Providers	ID.SC-2
15.2	Establish and Maintain a Service Provider Management Policy	ID.GV-2 ID.SC-1
15.3	Classify Service Providers	ID.SC-2
15.4	Ensure Service Provider Contracts Include Security Requirements	ID.SC-3 PR.AT-3
15.5	Assess Service Providers	ID.SC-4 ID.SC-2
15.6	Monitor Service Providers	DE.CM-6
15.7	Securely Decommission Service Providers	PR.AC-1
	Application Software Security	
16.1	Establish and Maintain a Secure Application Development Process	PR.IP-1
16.2	Establish and Maintain a Process to Accept and Address Software Vulnerabilities	RS.AN-5
16.3	Perform Root Cause Analysis on Security Vulnerabilities	RS.AN-1
16.4	Establish and Manage an Inventory of Third-Party Software Components	ID.AM-2
16.5	Use Up-to-Date and Trusted Third-Party Software Components	PR.IP-2
16.6	Establish and Maintain a Severity Rating System and Process for Application Vulnerabilities	RS.AN-1
16.7	Use Standard Hardening Configuration Templates for Application Infrastructure	PR.IP-1
16.8	Separate Production and Non-Production Systems	PR.DS-7
16.9	Train Developers in Application Security Concepts and Secure Coding	PR.AT-1 PR.AT-2
16.10	Apply Secure Design Principles in Application Architectures	PR.IP-2
16.11	Leverage Vetted Modules or Services for Application Security Components	PR.DS-1 PR.DS-2
16.12	Implement Code-Level Security Checks	PR.IP-2
16.13	Conduct Application Penetration Testing	
16.14	Conduct Threat Modeling	PR.AC-5 PR.DS-5 PR.DS-8 PR.IP-7

(Continued)

CIS Sub-Control	CIS Control	NIST CSF
	Incident Response Management	
17.1	Designate Personnel to Manage Incident Handling	PR.IP-9 DE.DP-1
17.2	Establish and Maintain Contact Information for Reporting Security Incidents	RS.CO-1
17.3	Establish and Maintain an Enterprise Process for Reporting Incidents	PR.IP-9 PR.AT-1
17.4	Establish and Maintain an Incident Response Process	ID.GV-2 PR.IP-9 DE.DP-1 RS.CO-1
17.5	Assign Key Roles and Responsibilities	DE.DP-4 RS.CO-2 RS.CO-3 RS.CO-4
17.6	Define Mechanisms for Communicating During Incident Response	
17.7	Conduct Routine Incident Response Exercises	PR.IP-10
17.8	Conduct Post-Incident Reviews	RS.IM-1 RS.IM-2
17.9	Establish and Maintain Security Incident Thresholds	RS.AN-4
	Penetration Testing	
18.1	Establish and Maintain a Penetration Testing Program	PR.IP-7
18.2	Perform Periodic External Penetration Tests	
18.3	Remediate Penetration Test Findings	
18.4	Validate Security Measures	
18.5	Perform Periodic Internal Penetration Tests	

Answers to Chapter Quizzes

CHAPTER 1

1. **When it comes to planning for how you will deal with cybersecurity risks, what are the first steps your organization should take? (Select One)**

   a. Form a working group across the organization's various departments (business, technical, legal, sales) to develop a plan. [Answer: Wrong. Although very important to how your organization manages risks, forming a working group of colleagues across your organization should occur later in the planning process after some key building blocks, such as building asset inventories, are completed.]

   b. Make a list of the vulnerabilities we know we have and start building our plan to address those vulnerabilities. [Answer: Wrong. Identifying your vulnerabilities is a crucial first step to conducting a risk assessment, but that comes later in the risk planning process.]

   c. Conduct an inventory of all our hardware and software assets. [Answer: Correct! As the saying goes, you can't protect what you don't know you have. The essential step in developing risk planning and management is to conduct an inventory of all IT- and IP-connected equipment and software.]

2. **Which of the following devices should you include in your asset inventory? (Select all that apply.)**

   a. Desktops, laptops, and servers. [Answer: Correct. Virtually all desktops, laptops, and servers have IP addresses and therefore are open to attack.]

   b. Mobile devices owned by the organization. [Answer: Correct. Virtually all modern mobile phones and computing devices have IP addresses.]

   c. Equipment specific to my organization connected to the internet or capable of being connected to the internet. [Answer: Correct. If these

Cybersecurity Risk Management: Mastering the Fundamentals Using the NIST Cybersecurity Framework, First Edition. Cynthia Brumfield and Brian Haugli.

devices can connect to the internet, they have IP addresses and are therefore vulnerable to attack.]

d. All of the above. [Answer: Correct.]

3. **How should you deal with outside IT or tech vendors or other third parties regarding access to your networks? (Select One)**

   a. I make sure that all third parties who have access to my networks comply with personnel security policies and procedures with which my own organization's employees must comply. [Answer: Correct. By using uniform policies and procedures for both employees and outside contractors, it's a lot easier to track and manage who has which kind of security level access to your systems.]

   b. Because the vendor is a leader in its field and many of my peers have recommended it, its cybersecurity policies are adequate to protect my organization. [Answer: Wrong. Even the biggest and best vendors might have security policies that conflict with your organization's needs. Examining their security policies is the only way to know if their policies match your own.]

   c. I limit access to my networks to only those IT or tech vendors I know well and have trusted in the past. [Answer: Wrong. Trust and familiarity are important components of any good relationship, but a more formal policy in terms of network access makes risk planning and management more comfortable to manage.]

4. **When briefing management and decision-makers on the cybersecurity risks your organization faces, which of the following is the best approach? (Select One)**

   a. Explain the risk planning and management processes we've developed in detail to inform these decision-makers fully. [Wrong: C-Suite executives and board members don't need to become experts on the nitty-gritty of cybersecurity. Briefings that convey the competitive aspects of the various risks your organization faces will be better absorbed and more effective.]

   b. Cut to the bottom-line to keep everything simple. [Wrong: Decision-makers need enough context and information to understand the competitive implications of cybersecurity risks.]

   c. Give them enough information to understand the competitive importance of cybersecurity risks and incorporate that understanding into business planning efforts. [Correct. Whatever methods you devise for informing management of risks, be succinct but make sure you touch on all the aspects of the dangers decision-makers need to know to make informed business decisions.]

5. **Which of the following is the best method for determining which assets rank highest in risk priority? (Select One)**

   a. Figure out where my organization is most vulnerable and rate those assets as the highest risk. [Wrong: Your organization's most vulnerable assets may not pose the highest risk. The goal is to focus on the most important assets that face the highest risk.]

   b. Figure out which assets get breached or attacked most and rate those assets as the highest risk. [Wrong: Bad actors may heavily breach some assets, but the risk level may be low if they're not important assets. Focus on the most important assets that face the most significant threats.]

c. Figure out the highest risk to important assets by factoring in those assets' vulnerabilities and the degree of threats they face. [Answer: Correct. Your cybersecurity risk planning should focus on the relative degree of vulnerabilities and threats for your most important assets.]

6. **Once you've figured out your highest priority risks, what is the best step toward managing those risks? (Select One)**

a. Develop a response plan to adequately deal with the risks and make sure I inform top management of this plan. [Wrong: Top management and all stakeholders in the organization should be part of the response plan's development to ensure an organization-wide perspective.]

b. Form a group of internal and external key players across the organization to help formulate a response plan and then perform regular assessments of the plan after it has been developed. [Correct. No response plan can be created in a vacuum, and it's important to include all the critical stakeholders in the organization in its development and ongoing assessment.]

c. Hire an outside cybersecurity firm to come up with a plan and help manage the risks. [Wrong. While outside cybersecurity experts can help the process, you need direct feedback from and participation of your employees, bosses, and peers throughout the organization from various departments to gain the best organization-wide perspective on handling cybersecurity risks that affect everybody.]

CHAPTER 2

1. **Which of the following made Major Motors' recovery from the attack take longer than it should have? (Select One)**

a. The company's databases were not adequately protected. [Wrong: Although protecting databases is very important to security, we don't know from the scenario what kinds of protection mechanisms, such as encryption, the company used.]

b. The company didn't use firewalls, or the hackers wouldn't have gained access to assets. [Wrong: Firewalls are essential for protecting the integrity of systems and data, but they are useless in situations where an attacker gains elevated admin access, in this case, super-user access, by stealing login credentials.]

c. The company didn't maintain at least some of its critical backup databases off site. [Correct: The attackers managed to destroy backup databases kept on the internal systems to which the attackers had access. If those databases had been stored securely off site or away from the company's operational systems, data restoration from those databases could have made the recovery process move more quickly.]

2. Which two essential steps in managing authorization credentials did the company miss?

a. The company failed to establish formal remote access procedures. [Wrong: We don't know from the scenario what the company's standard remote access procedures were. Moreover, the hackers gained Alan's super-user login credentials from his home computer, and there is no indication that Alan's home computer was used to access the company's networks.]

b. The company failed to maintain an up-to-date access control list that contains all of the authorization credentials and the individuals to whom these credentials apply. [Correct: Initially, Alan was overlooked as having a user account with super-user privileges because he appeared nowhere as a super-user on the access control list.]

c. The company failed to deauthorize Alan's temporary super-user account when it was no longer needed. [Correct: It had been weeks since Alan had been granted temporary super-user privileges, and yet his temporary account giving him those privileges was still active.]

3. Which of the following protective principles could have averted the company's disaster altogether?

a. The principle of least functionality. [Wrong: The principle of least functionality says that devices should serve the least functions possible with ideally one function per device. No system devices were implicated in the attack on the company.]

b. The principle of least privilege. [Correct: The principle of least privilege states that users should be able to access only the information and resources needed to do their jobs. Since Alan no longer needed to have super-user privileges to do his job, allowing him to have more expansive privileges gave the hackers the ability to move unhindered laterally across the company's systems.]

4. Which of the following access control policies *might* have averted hackers from attaining access to Alan's credentials? (Select One)

a. The company should have required Alan to use a VPN even while he was playing his video game. [Wrong: Although VPNs are beneficial to security when employees use remote access devices, they would not have helped in this circumstance. They would not have helped because a hacker had placed a keylogger on Alan's computer to gain access to his TeamTalk credentials, which unfortunately were the same as his super-user credentials.]

b. The company should have conducted a "health check" on Alan's computer if he had permission to work remotely using it. [Correct: Had the company established policies and practices for conducting health checks on employees' home computers or other privately used equipment, it's entirely possible – although not assured – that the keylogger on Alan's computer would have been discovered in time to avert the theft of his super-user credentials.]

c. The company should have segmented the network so that Alan couldn't access anything from his home computer. [Wrong: While segmenting the network is a useful protection measure in many circumstances, Alan can work remotely. It probably would not have been practical to segment his home computer from assets he needs to access in the course of his work.]

CHAPTER 3

1. **What is the first step in detecting anomalies that may indicate a cyberattack? (Select one.)**
   a. Develop a process within your organization for handling attacks and incidents. [Wrong: Although it's essential to develop methods for managing your organization's policies for handling anomalies and incidents, this development won't help you detect anomalies that can indicate a cyberattack.]
   b. Install an intrusion detection system. [Wrong: Intrusion detection systems are critical in detecting cyberattacks because they can help your organization respond more quickly and more dynamically, but they cannot on their own tell you what is an anomaly and what is not.]
   c. Establish baselines for determining what "normal" is and what is "abnormal." [Correct: It's impossible to establish mechanisms for detecting an anomaly without first knowing what "normal" traffic activity is and what are "normal" device configurations within your organization. Anomalies, or abnormal behavior, in how your systems operate are vital indicators of an attack.]
2. **Which of the following are some of the challenges in establishing an intrusion detection system? (Select all that apply.)**
   a. Staff may decide that some incidents that are alerted through the intrusion detection system aren't problems. [Wrong: After reviewing an alert sent by the intrusion detection system, staff may decide that the alert doesn't signify an actual problem. However, this is not a challenge in establishing an intrusion detection system.]
   b. Networks must continue to operate while intrusion detection systems run. [Correct: Any intrusion detection system might interfere with or slow down normal operations.]
   c. Intrusion detection systems often issue misleading messages. [Correct: Intrusion detection systems often give incorrect or false-positive messages.]
3. **If your organization can't establish network monitoring solutions for all systems and assets, which of the following should you do? (Select one.)**
   a. Rely on your intrusion detection systems to catch cyberattacks. [Wrong: Intrusion detection systems are essential because they enable dynamic searching for malicious changes, also called indicators of

compromise, such as IP addresses associated with malicious attacks, malware file names and hashes, and specific attack vectors. On the other hand, network monitoring solutions scan your systems and assets for abnormal changes, which can indicate cyberattacks.]

b. Run network monitoring solutions on those assets designated in your organization's risk assessment to be the most critical. [Correct: If your organization does not have the resources to run network monitoring solutions for all systems and assets, then prioritize which systems you should run monitoring on, namely those deemed most critical by your overall organizational risk assessment.]

c. Make sure to deploy antivirus systems that use host-based as well as network-based scanning. [Wrong: Antivirus software is crucial for keeping your systems secure by alerting you to the possible presence of malicious code and is a monitoring tool that can help detect attacks. But it is no substitute for network monitoring solutions that measure CPU utilization, network bandwidth, and other operations aspects.]

4. Which of the following are some of the key benefits of establishing detection processes? (Select all that apply.)

a. The event reports generated from these processes can yield insight into avoiding malicious attacks in the future. [Correct: By documenting the process for event detection, your organization might gain invaluable information into why the event happened and how to prevent it in the future.]

b. Event reporting that occurs under detection processes helps keep relevant personnel informed and foster better organizational communication. [Correct: By establishing a detection process and documenting that process in event reports, key security personnel stay better informed, and the organization as a whole has a shared understanding about that event and is better prepared to deal with similar events in the future.]

c. Detection processes help us evaluate the adequacy of providers' security practices. [Wrong: Although insight into providers' security practices could be a by-product of detection processes, that kind of evaluation should be undertaken by your organization's technical specialists and precede the establishment of detection processes.]

CHAPTER 4

1. Which of the following is the most useful first step in establishing a computer security incident response team – your CSIRT? (Select one.)

a. Review your IT personnel and select the best and brightest for inclusion on the CSIRT. [Answer: Wrong. Although you may be tempted to prioritize technical skills in responding to an incident, effect incident response should include a review of all the organization's personnel across all departments.]

   b. Develop an incident response plan and then figure out which personnel are essential to be on the CSIRT. [Answer: Wrong. You should develop the incident response plan after establishing the CSIRT to get useful input from across the organization, including information from top management.]

   c. Scan your organization to select CSIRT members from across the organization, including non-technical personnel. [Answer: Correct. Given that many different kinds of personnel will be impacted in a cybersecurity incident and will have a role to play, it's important to include on the team non-technical personnel from various functions, including legal, human resources, public relations, and other functions, depending on your organization.]

2. What is the most critical element in analyzing the cybersecurity incident? (Select one.)

   a. Prioritizing treatment of the incident. [Answer: Correct. Without knowing if the incident is a low, medium, high, or extreme damage incident, or in other words, without knowing how high a priority the incident is, it's virtually impossible to address it adequately.]

   b. Gathering and preserving evidence of the incident. [Answer: Wrong. Although it's essential to collect and preserve evidence to assist in possible criminal investigations and to shape better incident response in the future, gathering and preserving evidence is a lower priority than assigning a priority to the incident or exploring the who, what, when, where, and whys of the incident.]

   c. Examining your intrusion detection system. [Answer: Wrong. Although in most cases, reviewing your intrusion detection system will tell you what happened in the incident, it does not by itself give you a sense of how urgent the incident might be or how much organizational resources you should devote to responding to the incident.]

3. When it comes to mitigating cybersecurity incidents, which of the following steps will best help stop the incident from spreading through your organization? (Select one.)

   a. Eliminate the threat and block the adversary. [Answer: Wrong. Eliminating the threat and blocking the adversary is the goal of incident mitigation but might very well occur well after the incident has spread through your organization. The best approach to stopping the spread of the incident is first to contain it.]

   b. Take steps to contain the incident [Answer: Correct. After an incident has been reported and analyzed, it's essential to ensure that the problems caused by it don't compound the incident's damage by taking steps to limit the scope and magnitude of the incident within your organization.]

   c. Analyze the incident in hopes of finding its root causes [Wrong: Analysis of the incident is essential in mitigating cybersecurity incidents, but taking steps at the outset to contain the incident is the best step toward ensuring that it doesn't spread through the organization.]

4. **What does an incident recovery plan achieve? (Select all that apply.)**
   a. Helps the organization recoup or recover from any losses that may have occurred during the incident. [Correct: An incident recovery plan can help an organization take steps to address asset damage, such as hardware, or reputational damage, such as bad publicity.]
   b. Helps clarify whether the threat posed by the incident should be accepted, avoided, or limited. [Wrong: Classifying threats as acceptable, avoided, or limited should be a part of your mitigation activities and should precede incident recovery activities.]
   c. Helps the organization come to grips with the damage caused by the incident. [Correct: True disaster recovery can only occur when you have undertaken some assessment of the damage, an assessment that is aided by guidelines incorporated as part of the incident recovery plan.]

CHAPTER 5

1. **What should be your first step in managing supply chain risks? (Select One)**
   a. Establish processes for managing supply chain risks and assess their workability. [Wrong: Although establishing these processes and assessing their workability is close to being the first step you should take, the first step is actually to identify where the failure points are likely to be in your supply chain.]
   b. Communicate your organization's cybersecurity needs to your suppliers and their suppliers. [Wrong: Although communicating your needs to your suppliers and other third parties is crucial in managing supply chain risks, the first step you should take is to identify where the failure points are likely to be in your supply chain.]
   c. Determine where you need to manage those risks within your organization by assessing where the likely failure points might occur due to supply chain risks. [Correct: As is the case with most of cybersecurity risk management tasks, identification is crucial to managing supply chain risks – you can't manage what you don't know you have, as the adage goes.]
2. **Which of the following are important in addressing your suppliers' cybersecurity readiness? (Select All That Apply)**
   a. Communicate your organization's own risk assessment plan so that the suppliers can mirror your needs in drawing up the contract. [Correct: It's important to draw up the necessary provisions in your suppliers' contracts so that at a minimum they match your own level of security requirements.]
   b. Identify your suppliers and their partners and prioritize them according to the supply chain risk assessment processes you've developed. [Correct: Knowing who your suppliers and their partners are in terms of priority will better help you better manage resources and mitigate problems.]

c. Ask your suppliers to provide documentation and proof of their commitments to establishing and maintaining security. [Correct: By supplying documentation of their own security commitments, suppliers can help ease concerns about how seriously they take secure.]

d. All of the above. [Correct!]

3. **What should you do to ensure your suppliers can respond to and recover from service disruption? (Select One)**

a. Check to ensure that you give only authorized devices access and prevent unauthorized or unmanaged devices from gaining access. [Wrong: Checking to see that you give authorized devices access is important to confirm that your suppliers are meeting their contractual obligations, but is not part of gauging how well they will respond to and recover from service disruption.]

b. Examine physical and environmental controls to ensure the safety and security of supplier facilities. [Correct: Inspecting your suppliers' facilities to ensure their safety and security can ease your fears of how well they are poised to recover from service disruption.]

c. Rely on one-time statements or documentation from your vendors or contractors about their recovery plans. [Wrong: It's critical to continually assess the disaster recovery plans, security postures, and cybersecurity policies of your vendors and their partners. Don't rely on one-off statements because technology, software and, partnerships are fluid and constantly changing.]

Index

Indexer: Dr Laurence Errington.

Note: 'Q' indicates questions at end of chapters.

acceptance of incident 87
access control 4, 25–31,
    49, 50Q, 115
  monitoring access to physical
  environment 64
  PR.AC-1 27, 28
  PR.AC-2 28
  PR.AC-3 28, 29
  PR.AC-4 29, 30
  PR.AC-5 31
  PR.AC-6 32, 33
  PR.AC-7 33, 33–34
account management 27, 30, 115
activation
  of authorization, and deactivation 27
  of recovery plan 89, 90
active databases, protecting
  integrity 35–36
ActiveX 66
adaptive implementation xx
advocacy for more security by
  small organizations 112
alarm systems 64

alerts see reporting/notifica-
  tions/alerts
analysis 82–86
  RS-AN xix
  RS.AN-1 82, 83
  RS.AN-2 83
  RS.AN-3 84
  RS.AN-4 84, 85
  RS.AN-5 85, 86
anomalies and events xix, 74Q
  DE.AE-1 57, 58
  DE.AE-2 59, 60
  DE.AE-3 61
  DE.AE-4 61, 62
  DE.AE-5 62
antivirus software 60
appliances see devices/equip-
  ment/appliances
applications 118
  inventory 9–10
  prioritization based on importance 10–11
archived databases, protecting
  integrity 35–36

Cybersecurity Risk Management: Mastering the Fundamentals Using the NIST Cybersecurity Framework, First Edition. Cynthia Brumfield and Brian Haugli.
© 2022 Cynthia Brumfield and Brian Haugli. Published 2022 by John Wiley & Sons, Inc.

assessment/evaluation
  risk *see* risk assessment
  suppliers and third-party
    partners of suppliers
    99, 101–102
  see also testing
assets 113–114, 114
  configuration 114
  highest risk to *see* highest risk
  maintenance *see* maintenance
    and repair
  management (AM)
    xix, 4–13, 20
  identity in *see* identity
  monitoring *see* monitoring
  planning for asset continuity in
    a crippling attack or dis-
    aster 43–44
  threats and vulnerabilities
    posing highest risk to 17–18
  unauthorized (including
    devices) 6, 7, 8, 9, 67, 113
attackers and hackers 7, 16,
    23–24, 30, 35, 36, 50Q, 56,
    58, 63, 68, 72, 76, 76–77, 101
audit 28, 66–67
  logging 115–116
  supply chain risk manage-
    ment 101–102
authentication 25–33, 49, 66
  authorization and, dis-
    tinction 26
  based on risk involved in the
    interaction 33
authorization 26, 27, 28, 37
  activating and deactivating 27
  authentication and, dis-
    tinction 26
  credentials *see* credentials
  least authority possible 29–30
  of maintenance and diagnostic
    activities for third par-
    ties 45–46
  see also entries under
    unauthorized
automated tools or
    systems 16–17

patch management 42–43
software inventory
  tracking 9–10
for testing detection
  processes 71
avoidance of incident 87
awareness and training
    34–35, 117–118
  PR.AT-5 34, 35
  reviewers 60

backups 53
  forensic 86
banks 56–57
baseline configuration 41–42
  IT and OT Systems 40–41
baseline data for normal or
    regular traffic activity 57–58
Boswell, Jason 97
breaches *see* events
browser protection 116
bugs and flaws 68
  bug bounties 85, 86
  bug reports 85, 86
businesses
  continuity 43–44
  disaster recovery and, dis-
    tinction 88–89
  continuous monitoring 63

Carhart, Lesley 107
Casey, Ellis 85
CCTV (closed-circuit TV) 74
Center for Internet Security
    (CIS) Controls Version
    8.0 113–119
centralized log monitors 61
change management ledger
    (CML) 41
CIS (Center for Internet Security)
    Controls Version
    8.0 113–119
closed-circuit TV 74
cloud 6, 10, 32, 54
collaboration and coordination
    (in response)
  with management 79

with stakeholders 80, 81, 82
command and control master 58
committees
  information risk steering
  committee 14
  recovery recommittee 89, 90
communications 31, 71–72,
  80–81, 92, 103
  external 80–81, 92
  in incidents 58–59,
    71–72, 80–81
  in recovery (RC) xix, 91, 92
  in response xix, 80–81
  internal 31, 80–81, 92
  with peers 80
  see also collaboration and
    coordination
Communications Security,
  Reliability, and
  Interoperability Council
  (CSRIC) IV WG4 Final
  Report 111
computer security incident
  response team (CSIRT) 78,
  82, 83, 90, 93–94Q
confidentiality of corporate data
  outside internal networks,
  protection 36
configuration (system configuration and its management)
  41–42, 114
  logging devices 61
  standard configuration of
    network systems 57–58
consistency 19
  firewalls and 32
  response plans 81, 82, 84, 85
  in supply chain risk man-
    agement 97–98
containment of incidents 86–87
continuity
  business *see* business
  operational 79–94
continuous monitoring (security)
  xix, 62–68, 91
  DE.CM-1 63, 64

DE.CM-2 64, 65
DE.CM-3 65
DE.CM-4 65, 66
DE.CM-5 66
DE.CM-6 66, 67
continuous vulnerability management 115
contracts
  outside contractors 12, 21Q,
    38, 98, 104Q
  suppliers and third party
    contracts 100–101
control management function 70
  see also access control
coordination *see* collaboration
  and coordination
core (NIST framework) xvii–xviii,
  xxi
corporate data, protecting confidentiality and integrity
  outside internal
  networks 36
corporate-wide involvement in
  an attack 81–82
Council on Cybersecurity 15, 27
credentials 27, 28, 50Q
  identities proofed and
    bound to 32, 33
credit rating agency
  (Equifax) 42, 78
criticality (and critical elements) 81, 93Q
  in first response 79
CSIRT (computer security
  incident response team) 78,
  82, 83, 90, 93–94Q
CSRIC IV WG4 Final Report 111
Cybersecurity Council 15, 27
Cybersecurity Risk Management
  and Best Practices (CSRIC
  IV WG4 Final Report) 111

damage
  assessment 90
  limitation *see* limitation
  reputational 11, 38, 92

data
  corporate, protecting confiden-
    tiality and integrity outside
    internal networks 36
  flow *see* traffic
  protection *see* information
    protection
  recovery 116
  at rest 35, 36
  sent back to centralized log
    monitor 61
data security 35–39
  PR.DS-1 35, 36
  PR.DS-2 36, 37
  PR.DS-6 36, 38
  PR.DS-7 38, 39
decision-makers/making 3,
    13, 14, 21Q
defense
  malware 116
  recovery as last line of 89
  see also protection
detection xviii, 69–72, 74Q
  categories of Detect (DE) xix
  processes (DP) xix, 68–72, 74Q
  DE.DP-1 69
  DE.DP-2 70
  DE.DP-3 71
  DE.DP-4 71, 72
  DE.DP-5 72
  establishing 69, 74Q
  testing 71
  see also endpoint detection
    and response solutions;
    intrusion detection systems
development *see* establishment
    and development
devices/equipment/appliances
  internet-connected 7
  inventory 5–9, 20–21Q, 113–114
  network, standard configu-
    ration 57–58
  prioritization based on impor-
    tance 10–11

unauthorized assets and 6, 7, 8,
    9, 67, 113
  Wi-Fi-connected 7, 31
  see also hardware; media
DHCP (Dynamic Host
    Configuration
    Protocol) Logging 8
diagnostic activities for
    third parties,
    management 45–46
digital forensics 93
disasters *see* events
disclosures of vulnerabili-
    ties 85, 85–86
distributed denial-of-ser-
    vice (DDoS)
    attack 54
DNS (domain name sys-
    tem) 54, 58
documentation
  contracts with suppliers and
    third-party partners 100
  event detection 72
  vulnerabilities 88
domain name system
    (DNS) 54, 58
duties
  reviewer training in 70
  separation of 29, 30, 49
  see also roles and
    responsibilities
dynamic DNS 58
Dynamic Host Configuration
    Protocol (DHCP) Logging 8

education (about risk) 34
  managers 13–14
electronic monitoring
  employee behaviour relating to
    unauthorized access 65
  physical environment access 64
eliminating adversary
    immediately 87
emails

phishing 30, 34
    protection 116
    ransom 75–77
employees *see* personnel
encryption 37
endpoint detection and response
    (EDR) solutions 6, 10, 59, 63
end-user devices, inventory 5
Equifax 42, 78
equipment *see* devices/equip-
    ment/appliances
establishment and development
    detection processes 69, 74Q
    incident alert thresholds 62
    personnel security require-
        ments 11–13
    production environment kept
        separate from development
        environment 38–39
    supply chain risk
        management 98
evaluation *see* assessment/
    evaluation
events (breaches/incidents/
    disasters)
    alert thresholds, estab-
        lishment 62
    analysis *see* analysis
    communications with *see*
        communications
    definition/meaning 55–56
    detection *see* detection
    example scenarios 1–2, 23–24,
        50Q, 53–54, 75–76, 95–96
    impact *see* impact
    planning for assets and
        personnel
        continuity in a crippling
            attack or disaster 43–44
    recovery xix, 43, 44, 77, 89,
        90, 91, 92
    response to *see* response
    see also anomalies and events;
        hackers and attackers; threats
evidence-gathering and
    preserving 84

small organizations 112
    see also forensics
executable plans
    recovery 89–91
    response 79–80, 89–91
external communica-
    tions 80–81, 92
external parties and personnel
    12, 21Q, 59, 66–67, 73, 80
    contractors 12, 21Q, 38, 98, 104
    small business bringing in 112
    see also third parties
external threats 16–17, 69
    penetration testing 71

fail-safe 48
file integrating monitoring 37
firewalls 31–32
firmware, integrity checking 38
Flash 66
flash drive 46
flaws *see* bugs and flaws
forensics 84, 86
    digital 93
formal detection oversight 70
formal policies and practices 79
foundation, strong 57–58
free software 64
functional impact of incident 84

governance 13–15
    ID.GV xix, 13, 15

hackers and attackers 7, 16,
    23–24, 30, 35, 36, 50Q, 56, 58, 63,
    68, 72, 76, 76–77, 101
hardware 37, 113
    as asset 7, 8, 20, 113
    protection 37–38
    verifying integrity 38, 39
Hayslip, Gary 63
highest risk to assets
    developing plans for dealing
        with 18–20
    vulnerabilities and threats
        posing 17–18

home working 23, 26, 64
  and asset management 6
hot-swap 38
HTTPS protection 37
Hussey, Eric 89

identity (and identifying/identification) xviii
  categories of Identify xix
  ID.AM-1 xix, 5, 9, 10
  ID.AM-2 9, 10
  ID.AM-5 10
  ID.AM-6 11, 13
  ID.GV xix, 13, 15
  ID.RA *see* risk assessment
  ID.SC-1 98, 99, 100, 101
  ID.SC-2 99
  ID.SC-3 100, 101
  ID.SC-4 101, 102
  ID.SC-5 102, 102–103
  management 25, 28, 32–33
  proof of identity 32, 33
  supply chain risk management 98–99, 104Q
  threats 16–17
impact (of events/attacks) 56
  determination and assessment of 83, 84
implementation xix-xx
  of checking mechanisms to verify hardware integrity 39, 49
  for resilience achievement on shared infrastructure 48
  of review process 70
  small organizations 111–112
  tiers xix-xx, xxi
improvements (IM) in response plans 91, 92
incidents *see* events
industrial building systems connected to internet 7
industrial control systems 105–112
  baseline configuration 40–41

information
  access by only authorized persons 37
  backups *see* backups
  detection of incident 61, 71–72
  impact of incident on 84
  protection processes and procedures 39–44
  in recovery from incident, new 91–92
  verification of integrity 38
  see also data; documentation; reporting/notifications/alerts
information protection (data protection) processes and procedures (PR.IP) xix, 39–44, 114
  PR.IP-1 41
  PR.IP-3 41, 42, 43
  PR.IP-4 43
  PR.IP-9 43, 44
information sharing and analytics center (ISAC) 84
Information Systems Audit and Control Association's (ISACA's) RISK IT 15
information technology (IT) 55
  baseline configuration 40–41
  traditional 7, 8
infrastructure (network) 23–51
  management 116–117
  and planning 23–51
  shared, resilience 48–49
insurance 80
integrity
  checking mechanisms 37, 38, 39
  of corporate data outside internal networks, protection 36
  network, protection 31, 37
interactions
  authentication based on risk involved in 33

identities asserted in 33
intercepting adversary
    immediately 87
internal communications
    31, 80–81, 92
internal controls adequacy 66–67
internal threats 16–17, 69
internet
  appliance connected to 7
  industrial building systems
      connected to 7
  web browser protection 116
Internet-of-Things (IoT)
    devices 7, 8
intrusion detection systems
    58–59, 74Q, 82–83
inventory 5–10
  devices and systems
      5–9, 20–21Q
  software and applications 9–10
  updating 5–10
IP address 7, 56, 58, 62
ISAC (information sharing and
    analytics center) 84
ISACA's Risk IT 15

Java applets 66

Klein, Joe 26, 46, 47

laws and regulations 14, 81–82
  enforcement 94
  response plans and 81–82
layering entitlements when job
    functions change 26
leadership (leadership team)
    13, 70, 81
least functionality prin-
    ciple 47–48
least privilege principle 27,
    29, 30, 49
left of boom 55
limitation (of damage) 87
  reputational 92
load balancing 38
logs (and logging)

audit logs 115–116
centralized log monitors 61
of maintenance and repair
    activities 45

maintenance and repair (of
assets and systems) 44–46
  PR.MA-1 45
  PR.MA-2 46
malicious code and malware
  defenses 116
  software freedom from 65–66
managed security service pro-
    vider (MSSP) 13, 83
managers (management
    personnel) 1
  baseline 41
  briefing 21Q
  configuration managers 41
  education about risk 13–14
  response plan and collabora-
      tion with 79
  review reports for 70
  verification managers 41
manufacturing control sys-
    tems 105–112
Manufacturing Profile 106, 109
media (protection of)
  removable media 46, 47
  restricted use of certain media
      types 46–47
  storage media 37–38
medium-sized organizations *see*
    mid-/medium-sized
    organizations
mid-/medium-sized
    organizations
  implementation 111–112
  outsourcing 14
Miller, Patrick 4
mitigation 86–88
  RS.MI xix, 80, 93Q
  RS.MI-1 86, 87
  RS.MI-2 87
  RS.MI-3 88
  vulnerabilities 88

mobile code 66
mom-and-pop organizations *see* small organizations
monitoring and surveillance (security)
  continuous *see* continuous monitoring
  file integrating monitoring solutions 37
  of maintenance and diagnostic activities for third parties 45–46
  network 8, 63–64, 74Q, 117–118
  of risk on ongoing basis 3
MSSP (managed security service provider) 13, 83

National Telecommunications and Information Administration (NTIA) 97, 98
network(s)
  defining networking 29
  infrastructure *see* infrastructure
  integrity protection 31, 37
  internal, protection of confidentiality and integrity of corporate data outside of 36
  monitoring 8, 63–64, 74Q, 117–118
  roles and responsibilities regarding detection 69
  security controls 31
  standard configuration network devices 20, 57–58
  virtual private (VPNs) 29, 64, 67
New York State's Department of Financial Services (NY DFS) 81–82
NGO attack 53–54
NIST (National Institute of Standards and Technology)
  framework xv-xxi, 4–5, 25, 40, 42–43
  antivirus software 60

background xvi-xv
core/categories/subcategories xvii-xviii, xxi, 25
implementation *see* implementation
profiles xx-xxi, xxi
response planning 79, 84, 88
risk management *see* risk management
small organizations 111
supply chains and 96–97, 98–103
NISTIR 7621, Revision 1 111
non-governmental organization (NGO) attack 53–54
notification *see* reporting/notifications/alerts
NTIA (National Telecommunications and Information Administration) 97, 98

OCTAVE (Operationally Critical Threat, Asset, and Vulnerability Evaluation) 15
open-source software 64
operational continuity 79–94
operational technology (OT) 5, 40, 55
  baseline 40–41
Operationally Critical Threat, Asset, and Vulnerability Evaluation (OCTAVE) 15
outsourcing 13, 14, 45, 83
  see also external parties
ownership (of risk) 3, 19

partial implementation (of framework) xix-xx
patch management 42–43
Patton, Helen 34
peer communications 80
penetration testing 16, 18, 71, 119
personnel (staff; workforce; employees) and parties 11–13, 20

awareness and training *see*
    awareness and training
communication about events/
    incidents 58–59, 71–72, 80–81
external *see* external parties
    and personnel
layering entitlements when job
    functions change 26
managerial *see* managers
planning for their continuity in
    a crippling attack or dis-
    aster 43–44
security, establishment 11–13
third-party *see* third parties
trusted 112
unauthorized, monitor-
    ing 65, 67–68
phishing e-mails 30, 34
physical access to systems and
    monitoring of employee
    behaviour 65
physical environment, monitor-
    ing access to 64–65
physical protection 37
planning
    first steps 21–22Q
    recovery *see* recovery
    response *see* response
    risk 1–22
    user and network infra-
        structure 23–51
prioritization 18, 20, 21Q
    devices/software/applications
        based on importance 10–11
    suppliers and third-party part-
        ners of suppliers 99, 104Q
    of treatment (in response
        planning) 84
privilege (and privileged users)
    least privilege principle 27,
        29, 30, 49
    understanding of roles and
        responsibilities 35
production environment, devel-
    opment and testing environ-

ment kept separate
    from 38–39
protection xviii, 24–34, 50Q
    active and archived data-
        base integrity
        35–36
    categories of Protect (PR)
        xix, 25, 34
    corporate data confidentiality
        and integrity outside internal
        networks 36
    data *see* information protection
    emails 116
    hardware 37–38
    infrastructure planning and
        management and 24–34
    media *see* media
    network integrity 31, 37
    physical protection 37
    see also defense
protective technology 46–49

ransom e-mails 75–77
reconstitution and restoration
    phase of recovery plan 89, 91
recovery xviii, 50Q, 88–92
    ability to 84
    categories of Recover (RC) xix
    data recovery 116
    phases of recovery 89–91
    planning of recovery xix, 43, 44,
        77, 89, 90, 91, 92, 93Q
    executable 89–91
    importance 89
    in supply chain risk manage-
        ment 102–103, 104Q
regulations *see* laws and
    regulations
remote access to systems 28–29
repair *see* maintenance and repair
repeatable implementation xx
reporting/notifications/alerts
    in activation phase of
        recovery 90
    bug reports 85, 86

detected events 58–59, 71–72, 83, 90, 102
  examining and investigating of 82–83
  reviewing of reports 70
  thresholds, establishing 62
  see also documentation
reputational damage 11, 38, 92
resilience, shared infrastructure 48–49
response (treatment) xviii, 77–82, 119
  categories of Respond (RS) xix
  communications 80–81
  planning xix, 21Q, 43–44, 61–62, 77–82, 83, 84–85, 90, 92, 93–94Q
  executable plan 79–80
  in supply chain risk management 102–103, 104Q
  prioritization 84–85
  to risk 3
  see also endpoint detection and response solutions
restoration and reconstitution phase of recovery plan 89, 91
review of security 70
right of boom 55
risk
  accepted 88
  authentication based on risk involved in the interaction 33
  education *see* education
  highest *see* highest risk
  mitigation *see* mitigation
  planning 1–22
  prioritization *see* prioritization
risk assessment 3, 15–20
  ID.RA xix
  ID.RA-3 16, 17
  ID.RA-5 11, 17, 18
  ID.RA-6 18, 20
  meaning/definitions 2–3
  testing detection processes and 71
risk-informed implementation xx

Risk IT (ISACA) 15
risk management xvii, xix–xx, 1–10, 22
  cycle xxi
  process of 3
  strategy ID.RM xix, 18
  supply chain *see* supply chain risk management
Roberts, Bill 14
roles and responsibilities
  in network and security detection 69
  privilege and the understanding of 35
  in response 80–81
  see also duties

SaaS (software as a service) 6, 10
scenarios
  examples 1–2, 23–24, 50Q, 53–54, 75–76, 95–96
  testing 19
security group roles and responsibilities with respect to detection 69
security information and event management (SIEM) 61
Security Onion 64
security operations center (SOC) 13
security review 70
separation of duties 29, 30, 49
sequencing in execution phase of recovery plan 91
servers 47, 58
service(s)
  recovery from/response to disruption *see* recovery; response
  turning on only those needed 27
service providers 118
  external *see* external parties and personnel
sharing
  of evidence 84
  of infrastructure, resilience on 48–49

SIEM (security information and event management) 61
Singer, Omer 6, 57
skills training *see* awareness and training
small/mom-and-pop organizations
  implementation 111–112
  outsourcing 14
software (and software platforms) 113–114, 114
  antivirus 60
  bill of materials (SBOM) 97–98
  configuration 114
  free 64
  inventory 9–10
  malicious code *see* malicious code
  open-source 64
  prioritization based on importance 10–11
  SaaS (software as a service) 6, 10
  verification of integrity 38
  see also applications
staff *see* personnel
stakeholders (in response)
  coordination (in response) with 80, 81, 82
  supply chain risk management and agreement of 98–99
  third-party *see* third parties
steering committee (in risk management) 14
storage media, protection 37–38
suppliers 100–103
  developing contracts with 100–101
  identifying/prioritizing/assessing 99, 101–102, 104Q
  response and recovery testing 102–103
supply chain risk management 95–110
  first steps 98, 103, 103–104Q
  ID.SC-1 98, 99, 100
  ID.SC-2 99
  ID.SC-3 100, 101
  ID.SC-4 101, 102

ID.SC-5 102
special publication 800-161 96–97
surveillance *see* monitoring and surveillance
systems
  access control 27–28
  remote 28–29
  configuration *see* configuration
  inventory 5–9, 113–114
  maintenance *see* maintenance and repair
  monitoring *see* monitoring

tactics, techniques, and procedures (TTPs) 84
technology
  information, baseline *see* information technology
  operational *see* operational technology
  protective 46–49
testing
  backup systems 43
  detection processes 71
  penetration 16, 18, 71, 119
  production environment kept separate from testing environment 38–39
  response plan 80
  in supply chain risk management 101–103
  see also assessment/evaluation
third parties 21Q, 100–103
  developing contracts with 100–101
  establishing security 11–13
  identifying/prioritizing/ assessing 99
  maintenance and diagnostic activities 45–46
  off-site storage 36
  see also external parties
threats 16–18
  decreasing level of 87
  external 16–17, 69
  identifying 16–17
  internal 16–17

likelihood 17, 18
  determination 19
  posing highest risk to
    assets 17–18
tracking
  baseline data establish-
    ment and 58
  cloud applications 10
  software inventory 9
  suppliers and third-party part-
    ners of suppliers 99
traffic (data flow)
  analyzer 64
  baseline data for normal or
    regular 57–58
training *see* awareness and
    training; education
treatment *see* response
trusted personnel 112
TTPs (tactics, techniques, and
    procedures) 84

unauthorized assets including
devices 6, 7, 8, 9, 67, 113
unauthorized mobile code 66
unauthorized personnel/
    employee monitoring 6, 28,
    31, 46, 67–68
updating
  inventory 5–10
  recovery procedures 91–92
user and entity behavior analyt-
    ics (UEBA) 61
user planning and manage-
    ment 23–51

see also end-user
    devices; personnel

vendors 13, 32, 45, 60, 61, 67,
98, 99, 100
  patches 42
verification
  hardware integrity 38, 39
  managers responsible for 41
  software integrity 38
  source of anomalies 59
video monitoring 64
virtual private network (VPNs)
    29, 64, 67
virus protection software 60
voice-activated digital assistants 7
vulnerability and vulnerabil-
    ities 17–18
  continuous management 115
  disclosures 85, 85–86
  identifying 15–16
  to malicious code,
    assessment 65–66
  mitigation 88
  posing highest risk to
    assets 17–18
  scanning tools 68

Waters, Mike 80
weaknesses, detecting 55, 68
web browser protection 116
Wi-Fi connection 7, 31
workforce *see* personnel

Yu, Sounil 55